University Centre at

Black

Colleg

Telephone: 01

The Renaissance: Very Short Introduction

VERY SHORT INTRODUCTIONS are for anyone wanting a stimulating and accessible way into a new subject. They are written by experts, and have been translated into more than 45 different languages.

The series began in 1995, and now covers a wide variety of topics in every discipline. The VSI library now contains over 500 volumes—a Very Short Introduction to everything from Psychology and Philosophy of Science to American History and Relativity—and continues to grow in every subject area.

Titles in the series include the following:

Jerry Brotton

THE RENAISSANCE

A Very Short Introduction

OXFORD

UNIVERSITY PRESS

Great Clarendon Street, Oxford OX2 6DP

Oxford University Press is a department of the University of Oxford.
It furthers the University's objective of excellence in research, scholarship,
and education by publishing worldwide in

Oxford New York

Auckland Cape Town Dar es Salaam Hong Kong Karachi
Kuala Lumpur Madrid Melbourne Mexico City Nairobi
New Delhi Shanghai Taipei Toronto

With offices in

Argentina Austria Brazil Chile Czech Republic France Greece
Guatemala Hungary Italy Japan Poland Portugal Singapore
South Korea Switzerland Thailand Turkey Ukraine Vietnam

Oxford is a registered trade mark of Oxford University Press
in the UK and in certain other countries

Published in the United States
by Oxford University Press Inc., New York

© Jerry Brotton 2006

The moral rights of the author have been asserted
Database right Oxford University Press (maker)

First published as The Renaissance Bazaar 2002
First published as a Very Short Introduction 2005

British Library Cataloguing in Publication Data

Data available

Library of Congress Cataloging in Publication Data

Data available

ISBN 978-0-19-280163-0

16

Typeset by RefineCatch Ltd, Bungay, Suffolk
Printed in Great Britain by
Ashford Colour Press Ltd, Gosport, Hants

Contents

List of illustrations

The publisher and the author apologize for any errors or omissions in the above list. If contacted they will be pleased to rectify these at the earliest opportunity.

Introduction

An Old Master

National museums and art galleries are the most obvious places to go to understand what we mean when we talk about 'The Renaissance'. Most visitors to London's National Gallery fail to leave without seeing one of the most famous works of art in its collection – Hans Holbein's *The Ambassadors*, dated 1533. For many people Holbein's painting is an abiding image of the European Renaissance. But what is it that makes Holbein's painting such a recognizably 'Renaissance' image?

The Ambassadors portrays two elegantly dressed men, surrounded by the paraphernalia of 16th-century life. Holbein's lovingly detailed, precise depiction of the world of these Renaissance men, who stare back at the viewer with a confident, but also questioning self-awareness, is an image that has arguably not been seen before in painting. Medieval art looks much more alien, as it lacks this powerfully self-conscious creation of individuality. Even if it is difficult to grasp the motivation for the range of emotions expressed in paintings like Holbein's, it is still possible to identify with these emotions as recognizably 'modern'. In other words, when we look at paintings like *The Ambassadors*, we are seeing the emergence of modern identity and individuality.

This is a useful start in trying to understand Holbein's painting as an artistic manifestation of the Renaissance. But already some

1. Hans Holbein's *The Ambassadors*, an icon of the Renaissance, yet only discovered in the 19th century. Its enigmatic sitters and objects offer a wealth of insights into the period

rather vague terms are beginning to accumulate that need some explanation. What is the 'modern world'? Isn't this as slippery a term as 'Renaissance'? Similarly, should medieval art be defined (and effectively dismissed) so simply? And what of 'Renaissance Man'? What about 'Renaissance Woman'? To start to answer these questions, it is necessary to look more closely at Holbein's picture.

An educated Renaissance

What catches the eye as much as the gaze of both sitters is the table in the middle of the composition and the objects scattered across its upper and lower tiers. On the lower shelf are two books (a hymn book and a merchant's arithmetic book), a lute, a terrestrial globe, a case of flutes, a set square, and a pair of dividers. The upper shelf contains a celestial globe, and several extremely specialized scientific instruments: quadrants, sundials, and a torquetum (a timepiece and navigational aid). These objects represent the seven liberal arts that provided the basis of a Renaissance education. The three basic arts – grammar, logic, and rhetoric – were known as the *trivium*. They can be related to the activities of the two sitters. They are ambassadors, trained in the use of texts, but above all skilled in the art of argument and persuasion. The *quadrivium* referred to arithmetic, music, geometry, and astronomy, all of which are clearly represented in Holbein's precise depiction of the arithmetic book, the lute, and the scientific instruments.

These academic subjects formed the basis of the *studia humanitatis*, the course of study followed by most young men of the period, more popularly known as humanism. Humanism represented a significant new development in late 14th- and 15th-century Europe that involved the study of the classical texts of Greek and Roman language, culture, politics, and philosophy. The highly flexible nature of the *studia humanitatis* encouraged the study of a variety of new disciplines that became central to Renaissance thought, such as classical philology, literature, history, and moral philosophy.

Holbein is showing that his sitters are themselves 'New Men', scholarly but worldly figures, utilizing their learning in pursuit of fame and ambition. The figure on the left is Jean de Dinteville, the French ambassador to the English court of Henry VIII. On the right is his close friend Georges de Selve, bishop of Lavaur. The objects on the table are chosen to suggest that their positions in the worlds of politics and religion are closely connected to their understanding of humanist thinking. The painting implies that knowledge of the disciplines represented by these objects is crucial to worldly ambition and success.

The darker side of the Renaissance

Yet if we look even more closely at the objects in Holbein's painting, they lead us to quite another version of the Renaissance. On the lower shelf one of the strings on the lute is broken, a symbol of discord. Next to the lute is an open hymn book, identifiable as the work of the religious reformer Martin Luther. On the right-hand edge of the painting, the curtain is slightly pulled back to reveal a silver crucifix. These objects draw our attention to religious debate and discord in the Renaissance. When Holbein painted it, Luther's Protestant ideas were sweeping through Europe, defying the established authority of the Roman Catholic Church. The broken lute is a powerful symbol of the religious conflict characterized by Holbein in his juxtaposition of Lutheran hymn book and Catholic crucifix.

Holbein's Lutheran hymn book is quite clearly a printed book. The invention of printing in the latter half of the 15th century revolutionized the creation, distribution, and understanding of information and knowledge. Compared to the laborious and often inaccurate copying of manuscripts, printed books were circulated with a speed and accuracy and in quantities previously unimaginable. But the spread of new ideas in print, especially in religion, would also provoke instability, uncertainty, and anxiety, leading artists and thinkers to further question who they were and how they lived in a rapidly expanding world. This relationship between achievement and the anxiety it creates is one of the characteristic features of the Renaissance.

Next to Holbein's Lutheran hymn book sits another printed book, which at first seems more mundane, but which offers another telling dimension of the Renaissance. The book is an instruction manual for merchants in how to calculate profit and loss. Its presence alongside the more 'cultural' objects in the painting shows that in the Renaissance business and finance were inextricably connected to culture and art. While the book alludes to the *quadrivium* of Renaissance humanist learning, it also points towards an awareness that the cultural achievements of the Renaissance were built on the success of the spheres of trade and finance. As the world grew in size and complexity, new mechanisms for understanding the increasingly invisible circulation of money and goods were required to maximize profit and minimize loss. The result was a renewed interest in disciplines like mathematics as a way of understanding the economics of a progressively global Renaissance world picture.

The terrestrial globe behind the merchant's arithmetic book confirms the expansion of trade and finance as a defining feature of the Renaissance. The globe is one of the most important objects in the painting. Travel, exploration, and discovery were dynamic, controversial aspects of the Renaissance, and Holbein's globe tells us this in its remarkably up-to-date representation of the world as it was perceived in 1533. Europe is labelled 'Europa'. This is itself significant, as the 15th and 16th centuries were the point at which Europe began to be defined as possessing a common political and cultural identity. Prior to this people rarely called themselves 'European'. Holbein also portrays the recent discoveries made through voyages in Africa and Asia, as well as in the 'New World' voyages of Christopher Columbus, begun in 1492, and Ferdinand Magellan's first circumnavigation of the globe in 1522. These discoveries situated Europe in a rapidly expanding world, but also changed the continent's relationship with the cultures and communities it encountered.

As with the impact of the printing press, and the upheavals in religion, this global expansion bequeathed a double-edged legacy. One of the outcomes was the destruction of indigenous cultures and communities through war and disease, because they were unprepared for or uninterested in adopting European beliefs and ways of living. Along with the cultural, scientific, and technological achievements of the period came religious intolerance, political ignorance, slavery, and massive inequalities in wealth and status – what has been called 'the darker side of the Renaissance'.

Politics and empire

This leads to other crucial dimensions of the Renaissance addressed in Holbein's painting, and which define both its sitters and the objects: power, politics, and empire. To understand the importance of these issues and how they emerge in the painting, we need to know some more about its subjects. Dinteville and Selve were in England in 1533 on the orders of the French King Francis I. King Henry VIII had secretly married Anne Boleyn and was threatening to leave the Catholic Church if the pope refused to grant him a divorce from his first wife. Dinteville and Selve were trying to prevent Henry's split from Rome and act as Francis's intermediaries in the negotiations. So while this painting, like much of the history of the Renaissance, is about relations between men, it is noticeable that at the heart of this image is a dispute over a woman who is absent, but whose presence is powerfully felt in its objects and surroundings. The insistent attempts by men to silence women only drew more attention to their complicated status within a patriarchal society: women were denied the benefits of many of the cultural and social developments of the Renaissance, but were key to its functioning as the bearers of male heirs to perpetuate its male-dominated culture.

Dinteville and Selve were also in London to broker a new political alliance between Henry, Francis, and the Ottoman Sultan Süleyman the Magnificent, the other great power in European politics of the time. The rug on the upper shelf of the table in Holbein's painting is of Ottoman design and manufacture, suggesting that the Ottomans and their territories to the east were also part of the cultural, commercial, and political landscape of the Renaissance. Selve and Dinteville's attempt to draw Henry VIII into an alliance with Francis and Süleyman was motivated by their fear of the growing strength of that other great Renaissance imperial power, the Habsburg empire of Charles V. By comparison, England and France were minor imperial players: the terrestrial globe in the painting says as much. It shows the European empires beginning to carve up the newly discovered world. Holbein's globe reproduces the line of demarcation established by the empires of Spain and Portugal in 1494, following Columbus's 'discovery' of America.

This demarcation was made in response to a dispute over territories in the Far East. Both Spain and Portugal were struggling for possession of the remote but highly lucrative spice-producing islands of the Indonesian archipelago, the Moluccas. In the Renaissance, Europe placed itself at the centre of the terrestrial globe, but it looked towards the wealth of the east, from the textiles and silks of the Ottoman Empire to the spices and pepper of the Indonesian archipelago. Many of the objects in Holbein's painting have an eastern origin, from the silk and velvet worn by its subjects to the textiles and designs that decorate the room.

The objects in the bottom section of Holbein's painting reveal various facets of the Renaissance – humanism, religion, printing, trade, exploration, politics and empire, and the enduring presence of the wealth and knowledge of the east. The objects on the upper shelf deal with much more abstract and philosophical issues. The celestial globe is an astronomical instrument used to measure the stars and the nature of the universe. Next to the globe is a collection of dials, used to tell the time with the aid of the sun's rays. The two larger objects are a quadrant and a torquetum, navigational instruments used to work out a ship's position in both time and space. Most of these instruments were invented by Arab and Jewish astronomers and came westwards as European travellers required navigational expertise for long-distance voyages. They reflect an intensified interest within the Renaissance in understanding and mastering the natural world. As Renaissance philosophers debated the nature of their world, navigators, instrument-makers, and scientists began to channel these philosophical debates into practical solutions to natural problems. The results were objects such as those in Holbein's painting.

Finally, consider the oblique image that slashes across the bottom of the painting. Viewed straight on, it is impossible to make out the meaning of this distorted shape. However, if the viewer stands at an angle to the painting, the image metamorphoses into a perfectly drawn skull. This was a fashionable perspective trick, known as anamorphosis, used by several Renaissance artists. Art historians have argued that this is a *vanitas* image, a chilling reminder that in the midst of all this wealth, power, and learning, death comes to us all. But the skull also appears to represent Holbein's own artistic initiative, regardless of the requirements of his patron. It shows him breaking free of his identity as a skilled artisan and asserting the growing power and autonomy of the painter as an artist to experiment with new techniques and theories such as optics and geometry in creating innovative painted images.

Where and when was the Renaissance?

The Renaissance is usually associated with the Italian city states like Florence, but Italy's undoubted importance has too often overshadowed the development of new ideas in northern Europe, the Iberian peninsula, the Islamic world, south-east Asia, and Africa. In offering a more global perspective on the nature of the Renaissance, it would be more accurate to refer to a series of 'Renaissances' throughout these regions, each with their own highly specific and separate characteristics. These other Renaissances often overlapped and exchanged influences with the more classical and traditionally understood Renaissance centred on Italy. The Renaissance was a remarkably international, fluid, and mobile phenomenon.

Today, there is a popular consensus that the term 'Renaissance' refers to a profound and enduring upheaval and transformation in culture, politics, art, and society in Europe between the years 1400 and 1600. The word describes both a period in history and a more general ideal of cultural renewal. The term comes from the French for 'rebirth'. Since the 19th century it has been used to describe the period in European history when the rebirth of intellectual and artistic appreciation of Graeco-Roman culture gave rise to the modern individual as well as the social and cultural institutions that define so many people in the western world today.

Art historians often view the Renaissance as beginning as early as the 13th century, with the art of Giotto and Cimabue, and ending in the late 16th century with the work of Michelangelo and Venetian painters like Titian. Literary scholars in the Anglo-American world take a very different perspective, focusing on the rise of vernacular English literature in the 16th and 17th centuries in the poetry and drama of Spenser, Shakespeare, and Milton. Historians take a different approach again, labelling the period *c.*1500–1700 as 'early modern', rather than 'Renaissance'. These differences in dating and even naming the Renaissance have become so intense that the validity of the term is now in doubt. Does it have any meaning any more? Is it possible to separate the Renaissance from the Middle Ages that preceded it, and the modern world that came after it? Does it underpin a belief in European cultural superiority? To answer these questions, we need to understand how the term 'Renaissance' itself came into being.

No 16th-century audience would have recognized the term 'Renaissance'. The Italian word *rinascita* ('rebirth') was used in the 16th century to refer to the revival of classical culture. But the specific French word 'Renaissance' was not used as a descriptive historical phrase until the middle of the 19th century. The first person to use the term was the French historian Jules Michelet, a French nationalist deeply committed to the egalitarian principles of the French Revolution. Between 1833 and 1862 Michelet

9

worked on his greatest project, the multi-volume *History of France*. He was a progressive republican, vociferous in his condemnation of both the aristocracy and the church. In 1855 he published his seventh volume of the *History*, entitled *La Renaissance*. For him the Renaissance meant:

> ... the discovery of the world and the discovery of man. The sixteenth century ... went from Columbus to Copernicus, from Copernicus to Galileo, from the discovery of the earth to that of the heavens. Man refound himself.

The scientific discoveries of explorers and thinkers like Columbus, Copernicus, and Galileo went hand in hand with more philosophical definitions of individuality that Michelet identified in the writings of Rabelais, Montaigne, and Shakespeare. This new spirit was contrasted with what Michelet viewed as the 'bizarre and monstrous' quality of the Middle Ages. To him the Renaissance represented a progressive, democratic condition that celebrated the great virtues he valued – Reason, Truth, Art, and Beauty. According to Michelet, the Renaissance 'recognized itself as identical at heart with the modern age'.

Michelet was the first thinker to define the Renaissance as a decisive historical period in European culture that represented a crucial break with the Middle Ages, and which created a modern understanding of humanity and its place in the world. He also promoted the Renaissance as representing a certain spirit or attitude, as much as referring to a specific historical period. Michelet's Renaissance does not happen in Italy in the 14th and 15th centuries, as we have come to expect. Instead, his Renaissance takes place in the 16th century. As a French nationalist, Michelet was eager to claim the Renaissance as a French phenomenon. As a republican he also rejected what he saw as 14th-century Italy's admiration for church and political tyranny as deeply undemocratic, and hence not part of the spirit of the Renaissance.

Michelet's story of the Renaissance was shaped decisively by his own 19th-century circumstances. In fact, the values of Michelet's Renaissance sound strikingly close to those of his cherished French Revolution: espousing the values of freedom, reason, and democracy, rejecting political and religious tyranny, and enshrining the spirit of freedom and the dignity of 'man'. Disappointed in the failure of these values in his own time, Michelet went in search of a historical moment where the values of liberty and egalitarianism triumphed and promised a modern world free of tyranny.

Swiss Renaissance

Michelet invented the idea of the Renaissance; but the Swiss academic Jacob Burckhardt defined it as an Italian 15th-century phenomenon. In 1860 Burckhardt published *The Civilisation of the Renaissance in Italy*. He argued that the peculiarities of political life in late 15th-century Italy led to the creation of a recognizably modern individuality. The revival of classical antiquity, the discovery of the wider world, and the growing unease with organized religion meant 'man became a spiritual *individual*'. Burckhardt deliberately contrasted this new development with the lack of individual awareness that for him defined the Middle Ages. Here, 'Man was conscious of himself only as a member of a race, people, party, family or corporation.' In other words, prior to the 15th century, people lacked a powerful sense of their individual identity. For Burckhardt, 15th-century Italy gave birth to 'Renaissance Man', what he called 'the first-born among the sons of modern Europe'. The result was what has become the now familiar account of the Renaissance: the birthplace of the modern world, created by Petrarch, Alberti, and Leonardo, characterized by the revival of classical culture, and over by the middle of the 16th century.

Burckhardt says very little about Renaissance art or economic changes, and overestimates what he sees as the sceptical, even 'pagan' approach to religion of the day. His focus is exclusively on

Italy; he makes no attempt to see the Renaissance in relation to other cultures. His understanding of the terms 'individuality' and 'modern' also remain extremely vague. Like Michelet, Burckhardt's vision of the Renaissance reads like a version of his own personal circumstances. Burckhardt was an intellectual aristocrat, proud of his Protestant and republican Swiss individualism. He feared the growth of industrial democracy and what he saw as its destruction of artistic beauty. His subsequent vision of the Renaissance as a period where art and life were united, republicanism was celebrated but limited, and religion was tempered by the state sounds like an idealized vision of his beloved Basle. Nevertheless, in arguing that the Renaissance is the foundation of modern life, Burckhardt's book has remained at the heart of Renaissance studies ever since; often criticized, but never completely dismissed.

Michelet and Burckhardt's celebrations of art and individuality as defining features of the Renaissance found their logical conclusion in England in Walter Pater's study *The Renaissance*, first published in 1873. Pater was an Oxford-educated don and aesthete, who used his study of the Renaissance as a vehicle for his belief in 'the love of art for its own sake'. Pater rejected the political, scientific, and economic aspects of the Renaissance as irrelevant, and saw 'a spirit of rebellion and revolt against the moral and religious ideas of the time' in the art of 15th-century painters like Botticelli, Leonardo, and Giorgione. This was an aesthetic, hedonistic, even pagan celebration of what Pater called 'the pleasures of the senses and the imagination'. He found traces of this 'love of the things of the intellect and the imagination for their own sake' as early as the 12th and as late as the 17th century. Many were scandalized by what they saw as Pater's decadent and irreligious book, but his views shaped the English-speaking world's view of the Renaissance for decades.

Michelet, Burckhardt, and Pater created a 19th-century idea of the Renaissance as more of a *spirit* than a historical period. The achievements of art and culture revealed a new attitude towards individuality and what it meant to be 'civilized'. The problem with this way of defining the Renaissance was that, rather than offering an accurate historical account of what took place from the 15th century onwards, it looked more like an ideal of 19th-century European society. These critics celebrated limited democracy, scepticism towards the church, the power of art and literature, and the triumph of European civilization over all others. These values underpinned 19th-century European imperialism. At a point in history that Europe was aggressively asserting its authority over most of the Americas, Africa, and Asia, people like Pater were creating a vision of the Renaissance that seemed to offer both an origin and a justification for European dominance over the rest of the globe.

20th-century Renaissance

A far more ambivalent view of the Renaissance emerged in the early 20th-century. One of the earliest challenges to Burckhardt came in 1919, with the publication of Johan Huizinga's *The Waning of the Middle Ages*. Huizinga looked at how northern European culture and society had been neglected in previous definitions of the Renaissance. He challenged Burckhardt's period division between 'Middle Ages' and 'Renaissance', arguing that the style and attitude that Burckhardt identified as 'Renaissance' was in fact the waning or declining spirit of the Middle Ages. Huizinga offered as an example the 15th-century Flemish art of Jan van Eyck:

> Both in form and in idea it is a product of the waning Middle Ages. If certain historians of art have discovered Renaissance elements in it, it is because they have confounded, very wrongly, realism and Renaissance. Now this scrupulous realism, this aspiration to render exactly all natural details, is the characteristic feature of the spirit of the expiring Middle Ages.

The detailed visual realism of van Eyck's painting represents for Huizinga the end of a medieval tradition, not the birth of a Renaissance spirit of heightened artistic expression. While

Huizinga did not reject the use of the term 'Renaissance', there remained little left of the idea that he did not see emanating from the Middle Ages. Huizinga's book offered a very pessimistic view of the ideal of the Renaissance celebrated by his 19th-century predecessors. Written in the midst of the First World War, it is hardly surprising that it could summon little enthusiasm for the idea of the Renaissance as the flowering of the superiority of European individuality and 'civilization'.

The mid-20th century witnessed a profound reappraisal of the Renaissance by a group of Central European intellectual émigrés writing at a time when the rise of totalitarianism threatened to undermine the humane philosophical values of Renaissance humanism. German scholars, including Paul Oscar Kristeller, Hans Baron, and Erwin Panofsky, fled the rise of fascism in the 1930s and went into exile in the United States. Their subsequent work on the Renaissance was deeply affected by these events, and continues to influence contemporary studies of the period.

Hans Baron's *The Crisis of the Early Italian Renaissance* (1955) argued that one of the defining moments in Renaissance humanism emerged in Florence as a result of the second Milanese war (1397–1402). For Baron, the moment when the Milanese Duke Giangaleazzo Visconti prepared to attack Florence in 1402, resembled 'events in modern history when unifying conquest loomed over Europe'. Comparing Giangaleazzo to Napoleon and Hitler, Baron concluded that such modern analogies helped to understand 'the crisis of the summer of 1402 and grasp its material and psychological significance for the political history of the Renaissance, and in particular for the growth of the Florentine civic spirit'. Giangaleazzo was struck down by the plague in September 1402, and Florence was saved. For Baron, the great hero of what he characterized as the triumph of civic republicanism over feudal autocracy was the scholar and statesman Leonardo Bruni. According to Baron, in his *Panegyric to the City of Florence* and *History of the Florentine People*, Bruni expressed a 'new philosophy of political engagement and active life, developed in opposition to ideals of scholarly withdrawal'. This represented Baron's definition of civic humanism, which 'endeavoured to educate a man as a member of his society and state', and embraced the republican virtues which Baron saw represented by Medici Florence.

Baron's thesis was an attractive response to the role of the humane thinker at a time when Europe was threatened with the rise of political totalitarianism, and it decisively placed Florence and the Medici at the heart of the origins of the Renaissance. But it also idealized Bruni's humanism and Florence's republicanism. Paul Oscar Kristeller took a different approach to Baron. For Kristeller, it was the speculative philosophy of the Florentine humanist Marsilio Ficino, and in particular his *Platonic Theology* (written between 1469 and 1473), that defined a new fusion of the classical world and Christianity. For Kristeller, Ficino's innovation was the belief that

> philosophy now stands free and equal beside religion, but it neither can nor may conflict with religion, because their agreement is guaranteed by a common origin and content. This is no doubt one of those concepts with which Ficino pointed the way to the future.

Ficino's Platonism carefully negotiated the tense relations between philosophy, religion and the state – relations that were also particularly fraught in Europe in the 1930s and 40s when Kristeller was working on Ficino.

In the aftermath of the Second World War and the social and political upheavals of the 1960s, particularly the politicization of the humanities and the rise of feminism, the Renaissance was subjected to a profound reappraisal. One particularly influential response came from the United States. In 1980 the literary scholar Stephen Greenblatt published his book *Renaissance Self-Fashioning: From More to Shakespeare*. The book built on Burckhardt's view of the Renaissance as the point at which modern man was born. Drawing on psychoanalysis, anthropology, and social history, Greenblatt argued that the 16th century witnessed 'an increased self-consciousness about the fashioning of human identity'. Men (and on occasion women) learnt to manipulate or 'fashion' their identities according to their circumstances. Like Burckhardt, Greenblatt saw this as the beginnings of a peculiarly modern phenomenon. For Greenblatt, the literature of the great writers of 16th-century England – Edmund Spenser, Christopher Marlowe, and William Shakespeare – produced fictional characters like Faustus and Hamlet who began self-consciously to reflect on and manipulate their own identities. In this respect they started to look and sound like modern men. The painting that Greenblatt used to introduce his theory of self-fashioning was none other than Hans Holbein's *The Ambassadors*.

Greenblatt concluded that in the Renaissance 'the human subject itself began to seem remarkably unfree, the ideological product of the relations of power in a particular society'. Writing as an American, Greenblatt has subsequently explored both his admiration for the achievements of the Renaissance and his anxiety with its darker side, most specifically for him the colonization of the New World and the anti-Semitism found throughout the 16th century.

Despite the title of Greenblatt's book, he and others began to use the expression 'the early modern period' to define the Renaissance. The term came from social history and proposed a more sceptical relationship between the Renaissance and the modern world than the idealistic accounts of Michelet and Burckhardt. It also stressed the idea of the Renaissance as a period of history, rather than the cultural 'spirit' proposed by 19th-century writers. The term 'early modern' still suggested that what took place between 1400 and 1600 deeply influenced and affected the modern world. Instead of focusing on how the Renaissance itself looked back to the classical world, 'early modern' suggests that the period involved a forward-looking attitude that prefigured our own modern world.

The concept of the early modern period also enabled an exploration of topics and subjects not previously thought fit for consideration in relation to the Renaissance. Scholars like Greenblatt and Natalie Zemon Davis in her book *Society and Culture in Early Modern France* (1975) explored the social roles of peasants, artisans, transvestites, and 'unruly' women. As intellectual disciplines such as anthropology, literature, and history learnt from each other's theoretical insights, the focus on excluded groups and marginalized objects increased. Categories such as 'witch', 'Jew', and 'black' were subjected to renewed scrutiny, as critics sought to recover neglected or lost voices from the Renaissance.

Critics like Greenblatt and Zemon Davis were also influenced by late 20th-century philosophical and theoretical thinking, most decisively that of post-structuralism and postmodernism. These approaches were sceptical of the 'grand narratives' of historical change, from Renaissance to Enlightenment and into Modernity. Thinkers as diverse as Theodor Adorno and Michel Foucault argued that the humane, civilized values they identified as originating in the Renaissance had little response to or were even possibly complicit with the catastrophes of the political experiments of Nazism and Stalinism and the horrors of the Holocaust and the Soviet Gulags. As a result, few late 20th-century thinkers had any appetite for celebrating the grand cultural and philosophical achievements of the Renaissance. Instead, many historians began to analyse things and objects at a much more local level.

Similarly, everyday objects, meaningful to everyday life, but subsequently lost or destroyed, were invested with renewed importance. Instead of focusing on painting, sculpture, and architecture, scholars from various disciplines began to investigate how the material significance of furniture, food, clothing, ceramics, and other apparently mundane objects shaped the Renaissance world. Instead of seeing similarities, these approaches suggested the gulf between the Renaissance and the modern world. Objects and personal identities were not fixed and unchangeable, as

Burckhardt had implied in his celebration of 'modern' man: they were fluid and contingent.

The legacy of the Renaissance in the 21st century remains as contested as ever. Since the attacks on the USA in September 2001, the rhetoric of the clash of civilizations between east and west has taken its lead from the assumption that the Renaissance represented the global triumph of the superior values of western humanity. However, as we will see in the next chapter, the origins of the Renaissance were far more culturally mixed than these claims would suggest, and its impact spread far beyond the shores of Europe.

Chapter 1
A global Renaissance

One of the problems with the classic definitions of the Renaissance proposed is that they celebrate the achievements of European civilization to the exclusion of all others. It is no coincidence that the period that witnessed the invention of the term was also the moment at which Europe was most aggressively asserting its imperial dominance across the globe. In recent years, alternative approaches to the Renaissance from history, economics, and anthropology have complicated this picture, and offered alternative factors crucial to understanding the Renaissance, but which were dismissed by 19th-century thinkers like Michelet and Burckhardt as irrelevant. This chapter situates the Renaissance within the wider international world. It argues that trade, finance, commodities, patronage, imperial conflict, and the exchange with different cultures were all key elements of the Renaissance. Focusing on these issues offers a different understanding of what shaped the Renaissance. It also leads us to think of the creativity of the Renaissance as not confined to painting, writing, sculpture, and architecture. Other artefacts such as ceramics, textiles, metalwork, and furniture also shaped people's beliefs and attitudes, even though many of these objects have since been neglected, destroyed, or lost.

Another famous Renaissance painting that raises many of these issues is Gentile and Giovanni Bellini's painting *Saint Mark*

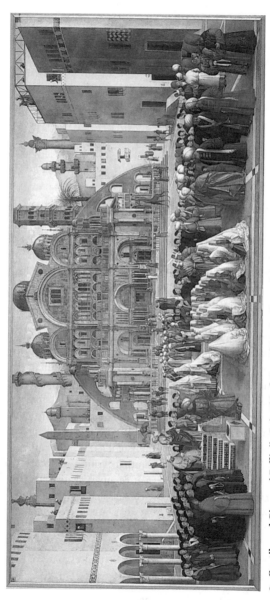

2. Gentile and Giovanni Bellini's *Saint Mark Preaching in Alexandria* (1504–7) captures Europe's fascination with the culture, architecture, and communities of the east

Preaching in Alexandria, the centrepiece of the Pinacoteca di Brera Renaissance collection in Milan. The Bellini painting depicts St Mark, the founder of the Christian Church in Alexandria, where he was martyred around AD 75, and patron saint of Venice. In the painting Mark stands in a pulpit, preaching to a group of oriental women swathed in white mantles. Behind Mark stands a group of Venetian noblemen, while in front of the saint is an extraordinary array of oriental figures that mingle easily with more Europeans. They include Egyptian Mamluks, North African 'Moors', Ottomans, Persians, Ethiopians, and Tartars.

The drama of the action takes place in the bottom third of the painting; the rest of the canvas is dominated by the dramatic landscape of Alexandria. A domed Byzantine basilica, an imaginative recreation of St Mark's Alexandrian church, dominates the backdrop. In the piazza Oriental figures converse, some on horseback, others leading camels and a giraffe. The houses that face onto the square are adorned with Egyptian grilles and tiles. Islamic carpets and rugs hang from the windows. The minarets, columns, and pillars that make up the skyline are a mixture of Alexandrian landmarks and the Bellinis' own invention. The basilica is an eclectic mixture of elements of the Church of San Marco in Venice and Hagia Sophia in Constantinople, while the towers and columns in the distance correspond to some of Alexandria's most famous landmarks, many of which had already been emulated in the architecture of Venice itself.

At first the painting appears to be a pious image of the Christian martyr preaching to a group of 'unbelievers', drawing on the classical world so precious to Renaissance thinkers and artists. However, this only tells one side of the story. Although Mark is dressed as an ancient Roman, in keeping with his life in 1st-century Alexandria, the garments of the audience are recognizably late 15th century, as are the surrounding buildings. The Bellinis depict the intermingling of communities and cultures in a scene that evokes both the western church and the eastern marketplace. The painting is a combination of two worlds: the contemporary and the classical. At the same time as evoking the world of 1st-century Alexandria and the life of St Mark, the artists are also keen to portray Venice's relationship with contemporary, late 15th-century Alexandria. Commissioned to paint a story of the history of Venice's patron saint, they depict St Mark in a contemporary setting that would have been recognizable to many wealthy and influential Venetians. This is a familiar feature of Renaissance art and literature: dressing the contemporary world up in the clothes of the past as a way of understanding the present.

West meets east

The Bellinis were fascinated by both the myths and the reality of the world to the east of what is today seen as Renaissance Europe. Their painting is concerned with the specific nature of the eastern world, and in particular the customs, architecture, and culture of Arabic Alexandria, one of Venice's long-standing trading partners. The Bellinis did not dismiss the Mamluks of Egypt, the Ottomans, or the Persians as barbaric. Instead, they were acutely aware that these cultures possessed many things that the city states of Europe desired. These included precious commodities, technical, scientific, and artistic knowledge, and ways of doing business that came from the east. The painting of St Mark in Alexandria shows how the European Renaissance began to define itself not in opposition to the east, but through an extensive and complex exchange of ideas and materials.

The Bellinis' Venetian contemporaries were explicit about their reliance upon such transactions. Venice was perfectly situated as a commercial intermediary, able to receive commodities from these eastern bazaars, and then transport them to the markets of northern Europe. Writing at the same time as the Bellinis worked on their painting of St Mark, Canon Pietro Casola reported with amazement the impact that this flow of goods from the east had upon Venice itself:

Indeed it seems as if all the world flocks here, and that human beings have concentrated there all their force for trading ... who could count the many shops so well furnished that they almost seem warehouses, with so many cloths of every make – tapestry, brocades and hangings of every design, carpets of every sort, camlets [sheets] of every colour and texture, silks of every kind; and so many warehouses full of spices, groceries and drugs, and so much beautiful wax! These things stupefy the beholder.

East–west trade in these goods had been taking place throughout the Mediterranean for centuries, but its volume increased following the end of the Crusades. From the 14th century Venice fought competitors like Genoa and Florence to establish its dominance of the trade from the Red Sea and the Indian Ocean that terminated at Alexandria. Venetian and Genoese trading centres and consuls were established in Alexandria, Damascus, and Aleppo, and even further afield. While Europe predominantly exported bulk goods such as textiles, timber, glassware, soap, paper, copper, salt, silver, and gold, it tended to import luxury and high-value goods. These ranged from spices (black pepper, nutmeg, cloves, and cinnamon), cotton, silk, satin, velvet, and carpets to opium, tulips, sandalwood, porcelain, horses, rhubarb, and precious stones, as well as vivid dyes used in textile manufacture and painting.

Their impact upon the culture and consumption of communities from Venice to London was gradual but profound. Every sphere of life was affected, from eating to painting. As the domestic economy changed with this influx of exotic goods, so did art and culture. The palette of painters like the Bellinis was also expanded by the addition of pigments like lapis lazuli, vermilion, and cinnabar, all of which were imported from the east via Venice, and provided Renaissance paintings with their characteristic brilliant blues and reds. The loving detail with which the Bellini painting of St Mark reproduces silk, velvet, muslin, cotton, tiling, carpets, even livestock, reflected the Bellinis' awareness of how these exchanges with the east were transforming the sights, smells, and tastes of the world, and the ability of the artist to reproduce them.

The eastern bazaars of Cairo, Aleppo, and Damascus were also responsible for shaping the architecture of Renaissance Venice. The Venetian art historian Giuseppe Fiocco described Venice as a 'colossal *suq*', and more recently architectural historians have noticed how many characteristics of the city were based on direct emulation of eastern design and decor. The Rialto market, with its linear buildings arranged in parallel to the main arteries is strikingly similar to the layout of the Syrian trading capital of Aleppo. The windows, arches, and decorative façades of the Doge's Palace and the Palazzo Ducale all draw their inspiration from the mosques, bazaars, and palaces of cities like Cairo, Acre, and Tabriz, where Venetian merchants had traded for centuries. Venice was a quintessential Renaissance city, not just for its combination of commerce and aesthetic luxury, but also for its admiration and emulation of eastern cultures.

Credits and debits

One characteristic of the Renaissance was a new expression of wealth, and the related consumption of luxury goods. Economic and political historians have fiercely debated the reasons for the changes in demand and consumption from the 14th century onwards. The belief in the flowering of the spirit of the Renaissance is also strangely at odds with the general belief that the 14th and 15th centuries experienced a profound period of economic depression. Prices fell and wages slumped. The impact of the outbreak of Black Death in 1348 only intensified these problems. However, one of the consequences of widespread disease and death, just like warfare, is often radical social change and upheaval. Such was the case in Europe in the aftermath of the plague. As well as disease, warfare ravaged the region. The Muslim–Christian conflict in Spain and North Africa (1291–1341), the Genoese–

Venetian wars (1291–9, 1350–5, 1378–81), and the Hundred Years War across northern Europe (1336–1453) disrupted trade and agriculture, creating a recurrent pattern of inflation and deflation. One consequence of all this death, disease, and warfare was a concentration on urban life, and an accumulation of wealth in the hands of a small but rich elite.

As in most periods of history, where some people experience depression and decline, others see opportunity and fortune. States like Venice capitalized on the growing demand for luxury goods, and developed new ways of moving larger quantities of merchandise. Their older galleys, narrow oared ships, were gradually replaced by the heavy, round-bottomed masted ships, or 'cogs', used to transport bulky goods such as timber, grain, salt, fish, and iron between northern European ports. These cogs were able to transport over 300 'barrels' of merchandise (one 'barrel' equalled 900 litres), more than three times the amount possible aboard the older galley. By the end of the 15th century the three-masted 'caravel' was developed. Based on Arabic designs, it took up to 400 barrels of merchandise and was also considerably faster than the cog.

As the amount and speed of distribution of merchandise increased, so ways of transacting business also changed. The complexity of balancing the import and export of both essential and luxury international goods and calculating credit, profit, and rates of interest sounds so familiar to us today that it is easy to see why the Renaissance is often referred to as the birthplace of modern capitalism. Just as Christian European merchants trafficked in the exotic goods of the east, so they incorporated Arabic and Islamic ways of doing business through their exposure to the bazaars and trading centres throughout North Africa, the Middle East, and Persia.

In the 13th century the Pisan merchant Leonardo Pisan, known as Fibonacci, used his commercial exposure to Arabic ways of reckoning profit and loss to introduce Hindu–Arabic numerals into European commerce. Fibonacci explained the nature of the Hindu–Arabic numerals from '0' to '9', the use of the decimal point, and their application to practical commercial problems involving addition, subtraction, multiplication, division, and the gauging of weights and measures, as well as bartering, charging of interest, and exchanging currency. While this may seem straightforward today, it is worth remembering that signs for addition (+), subtraction (−), and multiplication (×) were unknown in Europe before the 15th century.

The kind of Arabic commercial practice that Fibonacci borrowed from drew on earlier Arabic developments in mathematics and geometry. For instance, the basic principles of algebra were adopted from the Arabic term for restoration, *al-jabru*. Around AD 825 the Persian astronomer Abu Ja'far Mohammed ibn Mûsâ al-Khowârizmî wrote a book which included the rules of arithmetic for the decimal positional number system, called *Kitāb al jābr w'al-muqābala* ('Rules of Restoration and Reduction'). His Latinized name provided the basis for the further study of one of the cornerstones of modern mathematics: the algorithm.

Fibonacci's new methods were adopted in the trading centres of Venice, Florence, and Genoa. They realized that new ways of keeping track of increasingly complex and international commercial transactions were needed. Payment on goods was often provided in silver or gold bullion, but as sales increased and more than two people became involved in any one business deal, new ways of trading were required. One of the most significant innovations was the bill of exchange, the earliest example of paper money. A bill of exchange was the ancestor of the modern cheque, which originated from the medieval Arabic term *sakk*. When you write a cheque, you are drawing on your creditworthiness at a bank. Your bank will honour the cheque when the holder presents it for payment. A 14th-century trader would similarly pay for a consignment of merchandise with a paper bill of exchange drawn from a powerful merchant family, who would honour the bill when it was presented either on a specific later date, or upon delivery of the goods. Merchant families that guaranteed such transactions on pieces of paper soon transformed themselves into bankers as well as merchants. The merchant turned banker made money on these transactions by charging interest based on the amount of time it took for the bill to be repaid and through manipulating the rate of exchange between different international currencies.

The medieval church still forbade usury, defined as the charging of interest on a loan. The religious tenets of both Christianity and Islam officially forbade usury, but in practice both cultures found loopholes to maximize financial profit. Merchant bankers could disguise the charging of interest by nominally lending money in one currency and then collecting it in a different currency. Built into this process was a favourable rate of exchange that allowed the merchant banker to profit by a percentage of the original amount. The banker therefore held money on 'deposit' for other merchants and in return established sufficient 'credit' for other merchants to accept their bills of exchange as a form of money in its own right. Another solution was to employ Jewish merchants to handle credit transactions and act as commercial mediators between the two religions, for the simple reason that Jews were free of any official religious prohibition against usury. From this historical accident emerged the anti-Semitic stereotype of Jews and their supposed predisposition towards international finance, a direct product of Christian and Muslim hypocrisy.

The accumulating wealth and status of merchant bankers laid the foundations for the political power and artistic innovation characteristic of the European Renaissance. The Medici family who dominated Florentine politics and culture throughout the 15th century started out life as merchant bankers. In 1397 Giovanni di Bicci de' Medici established the Medici Bank in Florence, which soon perfected the art of double-entry bookkeeping and accounting, deposit and transfer banking, maritime insurance, and the circulation of bills of exchange. The Medici Bank also became 'God's banker' by transferring the papacy's funds throughout Europe. By 1429 the humanist scholar and Florentine chancellor Poggio Bracciolini argued that 'money is necessary as the sinews that maintain the state', and that it was 'very advantageous, both for the common welfare and for civic life'. Examining the impact of trade and commerce on cities, he could rightly celebrate the 'many magnificent houses, distinguished villas, churches, colonnades, and hospitals [that] have been constructed in our own time' with the money generated by the Medici.

East meets west

International trade and new financial practices shaped what people made and what they consumed throughout the 14th and 15th centuries. In 1453, the Hundred Years War between England and France ended. One consequence of the peace was an intensification of trade between northern and southern Europe. At the other end of Europe 1453 witnessed another equally momentous event. This was the year that the Islamic Ottoman Empire finally conquered Constantinople. Its fall to the Ottoman forces signalled a decisive shift in international political power. It confirmed the Ottomans as one of the most powerful empires in Europe and a player in shaping the subsequent art and culture of the Renaissance.

In the spring of 1453 over 100,000 troops laid siege to Constantinople, and in May Sultan Mehmed II captured the city. As the capital of the Byzantine Empire, Constantinople was one of the last connections between the world of classical Rome and 15th-century Italy. It acted as a conduit for the recovery of much of the learning of classical culture, thanks initially to the patronage of Sultan Mehmed. His affinity with the political ambitions and cultural tastes of his Italian counterparts led him to employ Italian humanists who 'read to the Sultan daily from ancient historians such as Laertius, Herodotus, Livy and Quintus Curtius and from chronicles of the popes and the Lombard kings'. If the Renaissance involved the rebirth of classical ideals, then Mehmed was one of its adherents. His library, much of which remains in the Topkapi Saray in Istanbul, surpassed those of the Medici and Sforza in Italy, and included copies of Ptolemy's *Geography*, Homer's *Iliad*, and other texts in Greek, Hebrew, and Arabic. He explicitly compared his imperial achievements to those of Alexander the Great, and saw himself as a new Caesar, with the potential to conquer Rome and unify the three great religions of the book – Christianity, Islam, and Judaism.

Like many other Renaissance leaders with aspirations to imperial power, Mehmed used learning, art, and architecture to magnify his claims to absolute political authority. He embarked upon an ambitious building programme that involved repopulating the city with Jewish and Christian merchants and craftsmen, founding the Great Bazaar that established the city's pre-eminence as an international trading centre, and renaming it Istanbul. He renovated the church of Hagia Sophia, transforming it into the city's first sultanic mosque, whilst at the same time hiring Italian architects to assist in the building of his new imperial palace, the Topkapi Saray. The new international architectural idiom, drawing on classical, Islamic, and contemporary Italian styles, aimed to produce what one Ottoman commentator called 'a palace that would outshine all and be more marvellous than all preceding palaces in looks, size, cost and gracefulness'. This international Renaissance style would also be recognizable to both Muslims and Christians alike, as confirmed by the Venetian ambassador, who praised the Topkapi as 'the most beautiful, the most convenient, and most miraculous [palace] in the world'. Like so many Renaissance buildings and artefacts, the Topkapi was both an original creative act and a highly political object. The two impulses were inseparable – a defining feature of the Renaissance.

Such international competition between eastern and western states and empires stimulated a whole new generation of Renaissance thinkers, writers, and artists. Many offered their services to

Mehmed, including the Venetian painter Gentile Bellini who painted a portrait of Mehmed that still hangs in the National Gallery in London. Bellini returned to Venice with gifts from Mehmed, and 'a chain wrought in the Turkish manner, equal in weight to 250 gold crowns'. In the painting of *Saint Mark Preaching in Alexandria*, at the foot of Mark's pulpit, is a self-portrait of Gentile; round his neck hangs the chain presented to him by Mehmed. Bellini proudly displayed the fruits of Mehmed's patronage, and used his experiences in Istanbul to add exotic detail to his depiction of Alexandria.

These exchanges quickly affected the style of what we now call Renaissance art. When the Italian artist Costanzo da Moysis also went to Istanbul to work for Mehmed, his paintings and drawings drew on the artistic conventions of Persian and Ottoman art. The pen and gouache drawing attributed to Costanzo, entitled *Seated Scribe*, is an intimate study of an Ottoman scribe, complete with Persian inscription in the top right-hand corner. The use of bright, flat colours and painstaking attention to the detail of dress, posture, and design, shows Costanzo's absorption of various principles of Chinese, Persian, and Ottoman artistic styles. The two-way exchange of influences can be seen in a remarkable copy of Costanzo's drawing attributed to the 15th-century Persian artist Bihzâd, entitled *Portrait of a Painter in Turkish Costume*, executed some years after Costanzo's drawing. Bihzād learns from his Italian contemporary, while subtly changing the scribe into a painter, shown working on precisely the kind of Islamic portrait originally copied by Costanzo. Each artist draws on the aesthetic innovations of the other, making it impossible to say which painting is definably 'western' or 'eastern'.

The accession of Sultan Süleyman the Magnificent in 1520 intensified artistic and diplomatic exchanges. Süleyman commissioned grand tapestries from Flemish weavers, jewellery and an imperial crown from Venetian goldsmiths that he wore whilst laying siege to Vienna in 1532, and commissioned the great

3. **Costanzo da Moysis's exquisite** *Seated Scribe*

Ottoman architect Mimar Koca Sinan to build a series of palaces, mosques, and bridges to rival those of his Italian counterparts. Sinan drew on Turko-Islamic architectural traditions as well as the Byzantine heritage provided by the great church of Hagia Sophia to produce a series of mosques in Istanbul with domed central plans in the early 16th century. When Pope Julius II employed the architects

4. The Persian master Bihzâd's *Portrait of a Painter*

Donato Bramante and later Michelangelo to rebuild St Peter's in Rome, their designs drew on Hagia Sophia, with its half-domes and minaret towers, as well as Sinan's mosques and palaces. Both Ottoman and Italian architects were competing to rebuild their imperial cities by drawing on a shared intellectual and aesthetic tradition.

What such exchanges and rivalries suggest is that there were no clear geographical or political barriers between east and west in the Renaissance. It is a much later, 19th-century belief in the absolute cultural and political separation of the Islamic east and Christian west that has obscured the easy exchange of trade and ideas between these two cultures. The two sides were often in religious and military conflict with each other. However, the point is that material and commercial exchanges between them carried on in spite of these conflicts, and produced a fertile environment for cultural achievements on both sides. Their shared cultural heritage of a contested classical past led to new achievements that we now recognize as typically Renaissance.

The winds of change

Rather than shutting off cultural contact between east and west, once it was in control of Constantinople the Ottoman Empire simply placed a levy on such exchanges. The Ottoman authorities taxed the overland trade routes into Persia, Central Asia, and China, but this just created new ways of doing business. The end of the Hundred Years War stimulated a greater circulation of trade between northern and southern Europe, intensifying the demand for exotic goods from the east. This accelerated the scale of commercial exchange, and led Christian European states to seek ways of circumventing heavy tariffs. Most eastern merchandise was paid for in European gold and silver bullion. As the ore mines in Central Europe began to run dry and tariffs escalated, new sources of revenue were needed: this led directly to an increase in exploration and discovery.

For centuries gold had trickled into Europe via North Africa and the trans-Saharan caravan routes. Gold from the mines of Sudan was moved along these routes to Tunis, Cairo, and Alexandria, where Italian merchants exchanged it for European goods. From the beginning of the 15th century the Portuguese crown and merchants realized that seaborne travel along the African coastline could tap into these gold and spice markets at source, circumventing taxes imposed on overland trade routes through Ottoman territories. Such an ambitious project involved organization and capital. By the mid-15th century German, Florentine, Genoese, and Venetian merchants were sponsoring Portuguese voyages down the coast of West Africa and offering the Portuguese king a percentage of any profits.

However, it was not only gold that flowed back into Europe through these African trade routes. While travelling through the kingdom of a chieftain called 'Budomel' in southern Senegal, the Venetian merchant Alvise Cadamosto traded seven horses 'which together had cost me originally about three hundred ducats' for 100 slaves. For the Venetian this was a profitable deal, based on an accepted exchange rate of nine to fourteen slaves for one horse (it is estimated that at this time Venice had a population of over 3,000 slaves). Writing in 1446, Cadamosto estimated that 1,000 slaves were shipped from the region of Arguim every year. They were taken to Lisbon and sold throughout Europe. This trade represents one of the darkest sides of the European Renaissance, and marked the beginnings of a trans-Atlantic slave trade that was to bring misery and suffering to millions of Africans over subsequent centuries. It is sobering to note how the economies funding the great cultural achievements of the Renaissance were profiting by this unscrupulous trade in human lives.

The African gold, pepper, cloth, and slaves that flowed back into mainland Europe, alongside the merchandise imported from the east also sowed the seeds of a global understanding of the early modern world. In 1492, on the eve of Columbus's first voyage to the

New World, the German cloth merchant Martin Behaim created an object that encompassed the fusion of global economics and artistic innovation that was becoming increasingly characteristic of the time. This was the first known terrestrial globe of the world. Illustrated with over 1,100 place names and 48 miniatures of kings and rulers, Behaim's globe also contained legends describing merchandise, commercial practices, and trade routes. The globe was a commercial map of the Renaissance world, created by someone who was both a merchant and a geographer. Behaim recorded his own commercial experiences in West Africa between

5. The first modern terrestrial globe, made in Nuremberg in 1492 by the German merchant Martin Behaim following his return from West Africa

6. An early 16th-century Bini-Portuguese salt cellar, designed by Portuguese travellers, carved by African craftsmen: the result is a completely new Renaissance art object

1482 and 1484, and they give some indication of what motivated his voyages. He sailed 'with various goods and merchandise for sale and barter', including horses 'to be presented to Moorish kings', as well as 'various examples of spices to be shown to the Moors in order that they might understand what we sought in their country'. Spices, gold, and slaves: these commodities underpinned the creation of the first truly global image of the Renaissance world.

Such cultural and commercial influences were not all one-way. One Portuguese chronicler noted that, 'in Sierra Leone, men are very clever and make extremely beautiful objects such as spoons, salt cellars, and dagger hilts'. This is a direct reference to the 'Afro-Portuguese ivories'. Carved by African artists from Sierra Leone and Nigeria, these beautiful artworks fuse African style with European motifs to create a hybrid object that is unique to both cultures. Salt cellars and oliphants (hunting horns) were particularly common examples of such carvings, and were owned by figures like Albrecht Dürer and the Medici family. One particularly striking salt cellar, dated to the early 16th century, depicts four Portuguese figures supporting a basket upon which sails a Portuguese ship. With an added touch of humour a sailor peeps out from the crow's nest. The details of the clothing, weapons, and rigging are obviously drawn from detailed observation of and encounters with Portuguese seafarers. Scholars believe that these carvings were designed for export to Europe. The delicate beaded, braided, and twisted features of these carvings heavily influenced the architecture of 16th-century Portugal as it began to raise monuments celebrating its commercial power in Africa and the Far East.

Chapter 2
The humanist script

In November 1466 George of Trebizond, one of the most celebrated humanist scholars of the 15th century, found himself languishing in a Roman jail on the orders of Pope Paul II. Since his arrival in Venice as a Greek-speaking scholar 50 years earlier, George had established himself as a brilliant practitioner of the new intellectual and educational arts of the day, inspired by the classical authors of Greece and Rome. Utilizing his skills in Greek and Latin, he rapidly rose to prominence with the publication of textbooks on rhetoric and logic, and commentaries and translations of Aristotle and Plato.

By 1450 George was papal secretary and leading lecturer in the new humanities curriculum, the so-called *studia humanitatis*, at the Studio Romano, under the patronage of Pope Nicholas V. However, younger humanist scholars began to criticize George's translations. In 1465 George headed for Mehmed the Conqueror's new capital of Istanbul, formerly Constantinople. Knowing Mehmed's scholarly interests, George wrote a preface to the classical Greek geographer Ptolemy that he dedicated to the sultan, 'thinking that there is nothing better in the present life than to serve a wise king and one who philosophizes about the greatest matters'. George also dedicated his comparison of Aristotle and Plato to the sultan, and returned to Rome to compose a series of letters to Mehmed, claiming that 'there has never been a man nor will there ever be one to whom God has granted a greater opportunity for sole dominion of the world'. In his rhetorically powerful letters and dedications George apparently saw Mehmed as a suitable patron of his academic skills. Upon learning of his intellectual flirtation with the sultan, the pope wasn't impressed and imprisoned George. His incarceration was brief and, after a stint in Budapest, he returned to Rome to witness his books on rhetoric and dialectic receive a new lease of life as a result of their distribution via a new invention: the printing press.

This chapter examines the rise of one of the most complex and controversial of all philosophical terms, Renaissance humanism, and its close relationship to one of the most important technological developments of the pre-modern world, the invention of the printing press. What united these two developments was the book. At the beginning of the 15th century, literacy and books were the preserve of a tiny, international elite focused on urban centres like Constantinople, Baghdad, Rome, and Venice. By the end of the 16th century humanism and the printing press had created a revolution in both elite and popular apprehensions of reading, writing, and the status of knowledge, transmitted via the printed book, which became focused much more exclusively on northern Europe.

George of Trebizond's career spans a defining moment for both intellectual thought and the history of the book. This was a time when a whole generation of intellectuals developed a new method of learning derived from classical Greek and Roman authors, called *studia humanitatis*. These scholars fashioned themselves 'humanists' and engaged in an immense undertaking to understand, translate, publish, and teach the texts of the past as a means of understanding and transforming their own present. Renaissance humanism gradually replaced the medieval scholastic tradition from which it emerged. It systematically promoted the study of classical works as the key to the creation of the successful, cultivated, civilized individual who used these skills to succeed within the everyday world of politics, trade, and religion.

Humanism's success lay in its claim to offer two things to its followers. First, it fostered a belief that the mastery of the classics made you a better, more 'humane' person, able to reflect on the moral and ethical problems that the individual faced in relation to his/her social world. Secondly, it convinced students and employers that the study of classical texts provided the practical skills necessary for a future career as an ambassador, lawyer, priest, or secretary within the layers of bureaucratic administration that began to emerge throughout 15th-century Europe. Humanist training in translation, letter-writing, and public speaking was viewed as a highly marketable education for those who wanted to enter the ranks of the social elite.

This sounds a long way from the romantic, idealized picture of humanists rescuing the great books of classical culture and absorbing their wisdom in creating a civilized society. It is. Renaissance humanism had a pragmatic aim to supply a framework for professional advancement, in particular to prepare men for government. A modern humanities education is constructed on the same model (the term is itself drawn from the Latin *studia humanitatis*). It promises the same benefits, and arguably retains the same flaws. It relies on the assumption that a non-vocational study of the liberal arts makes you a more civilized person, and gives you the linguistic and rhetorical skills required to succeed in the workplace. However, there are abiding tensions built into this assumption, tensions that can be traced back to Renaissance humanism.

Many of these conflicts can be traced in the career of George of Trebizond. It reveals that the development of Renaissance humanism was an intellectually gruelling practical business that involved painstaking detection, translation, editing, publication, and teaching of classical texts. George's combination of writing, translating, and teaching suggests that the success of humanism was mainly achieved within the classroom as a practical preparation for employment. New curricula and methods of teaching the demanding skills required of a humanist education were introduced. Humanism relied upon the creation of an academic community to teach and disseminate its ideas, but its members also quarrelled over the nature and direction of humanism's development, leading to the kind of vicious disputes and bitter rivalries that George experienced, and which compromised his career. Humanism marketed its skills to a governing elite that was persuaded to value the linguistic, rhetorical, and administrative expertise that a humanist education provided.

However, this promotion of humanism could often run into problems, as George discovered in his attempt to transfer his intellectual allegiance and humanistic skills from one powerful patron (Pope Paul II) to another (Mehmed the Conqueror). As a result, humanism concentrated its efforts on disseminating its method through the classroom and the revolutionary medium of the printing press. Humanism's alliance with print allowed scholars to distribute standardized copies of their publications in vast numbers way beyond the reproductive possibilities of scribal manuscript production. The impact of this association was a subsequent rise in both literacy and schools, creating an unprecedented emphasis on education as a tool of socialization.

The persuaders

The story of Renaissance humanism begins with the 14th-century Italian writer and scholar Petrarch. He was closely associated with the papal residency in Avignon in France, where his father was employed as a notary – a scholar skilled in the art of administering the mass of documents created by papal business. Petrarch drew on these scholarly traditions in his interest in the rhetorical and stylistic qualities of a range of neglected classical Roman writers, particularly Cicero, Livy, and Virgil. He began piecing together texts like Livy's *History of Rome*, collating different manuscript fragments, correcting corruptions in the language, and imitating its style in writing a more linguistically fluent and rhetorically persuasive form of Latin.

Petrarch also scoured libraries and monasteries for classical texts, and in 1333 discovered a manuscript of a speech by the Roman statesman and orator Cicero, the *Oration for Archias* (*Pro Archia*) that discussed the virtues 'de studiis humanitatis'. Petrarch described the speech as 'full of wonderful compliments to poets'. Cicero was crucial to Petrarch and the subsequent development of humanism because he offered a new way of thinking about how the cultured individual united the philosophical and contemplative side of life with its more active and public dimension. In his famous text *On the Orator* (*De Oratore*), Cicero posed this problem by contrasting rhetoric and oratory with philosophy. For Cicero, 'the whole art of oratory lies open to the view, and is concerned in some measure with the common practice, custom, and speech of mankind'. Philosophy, on the other hand, involved private contemplation away 'from public interests', in fact divorced 'from any kind of business'. Petrarch took up Cicero's distinction in his treatise *The Solitary Life* (*De Vita Solitaria*) in his discussion of the role of the philosopher and the role of the orator:

> Both the diversity of their ways of life and the wholly opposed ends for which they have worked make me believe that philosophers have always thought differently from orators. For the latter's efforts are directed toward gaining the applause of the crowd, while the former strive – if their declarations are not false – to know themselves, to return the soul to itself, and to despise empty glory.

This was the blueprint for Petrarch's humanism: the unification of the philosophical quest for individual truth, and the practical ability to function effectively in society through the use of rhetoric and persuasion. To obtain the perfect balance the civilized individual needed rigorous training in the disciplines of the *studia humanitatis*, namely grammar, rhetoric, poetry, history, and moral philosophy.

This was a brilliant argument for giving the early humanists greater power and prestige than their scholastic predecessors had ever enjoyed. Medieval scholasticism had trained students in Latin, letter-writing, and philosophy, but its teachers and thinkers were generally subservient to the authorities (usually the church) for which they worked. Cicero's definition of the civilized humanist, able to philosophize on humanity while also training the elite in the skills of public oratory and persuasion, gave humanism and its practitioners greater autonomy to 'sell' their ideas to social and political institutions. However, humanism was never an explicitly political movement, although some of its practitioners were quite happy to allow its approach to be appropriated by political ideologies as and where this proved beneficial. Humanists styled themselves as orators and rhetoricians, gurus of style rather than politics. It is often a mistake to take the subject matter of humanist writing at face value. Such writings were highly formal exercises in style and rhetoric, often delighting in dialectically arguing for and against a particular topic. Humanism's triumph lay in its ability to utilize its skills in rhetoric, oratory, and dialectic to convince a range of potential political paymasters of the usefulness of its services, be they republican or monarchical.

Back to the drawing board

By the mid-15th century the practice of humanism was spreading throughout schools, universities, and courts. Its emphasis on rhetoric and language elevated the status of the book as a material and intellectual object. Humanism's revisions of how to speak, translate, read, and even write Latin all focused on the book as the perfect portable object through which to disseminate these ideas. But how did these humanist ideals work in practice? One particularly vivid example of the gulf between the theory of humanism and its practice in the classroom emerges from the career of one of the most respected of all humanist teachers, Guarino Guarini of Verona (1374–1460). Guarino was employed by the Este dynasty in Ferrara, where he lectured as Professor of Rhetoric from 1436.

Guarino's success as a teacher rested on his ability to sell to both his students and his patrons a vision of humanist education that combined civilized humane values with practical social skills crucial to social advancement. In one introductory lecture on Cicero, Guarino asked:

> What better goal can there be for our thoughts and efforts than the arts, precepts, and studies by which we come to guide, order, and govern ourselves, our households, and our political offices [?] . . . Therefore continue as you have begun, excellent youths and gentlemen, and work at these Ciceronian studies which fill our city with well-founded hope in you, and which bring honour and pleasure to you.

This was a vision disseminated by a group of teachers and scholars trained in the art of rhetoric and persuasion; no wonder it was accepted so readily in its day, and continues to influence humanities students today.

However, Guarino's classroom did not necessarily produce the humane, elite citizens he promised. His education involved a gruelling immersion in grammar and rhetoric, based on diligent note-taking, rote learning of texts, oral repetition, and rhetorical imitation in a seemingly endless round of basic exercises. There was little time for more philosophical reflection on the nature of the texts under analysis, and students' lecture notes reveal only a very basic grasp of the new ways of speaking and writing that humanists like Guarino believed were the basis of humanist education. These elementary lessons in language and rhetoric did prepare students for basic employment in legal, political, and religious positions, although this was a long way from the exalted heights promised by Guarino in his introductory lectures.

Guarino's methods delighted his political patrons. The repetitious drilling of students in the fine points of grammar cultivated passivity, obedience, and docility. When this failed, discipline and correction were routinely implemented. Guarino also encouraged subservience towards the politics of the ruling elite, be they republican or (as in the case of his own patrons, the Este) monarchical:

> Whatever the ruler may decree must be accepted with a calm mind and the appearance of pleasure. For men who can do this are dear to rulers, make themselves and their relatives prosperous, and win high promotion.

For most humanist students, the rhetorical claims of humanism towards a new conception of the individual led in practice to employment in the foundations of the emerging bureaucratic state. Guarino ensured that political acquiescence matched the practical skills required for such positions. This guaranteed ongoing elite sponsorship of schools and universities that disseminated the ideals of humanism.

A woman's place is in the humanist's home

From humanism's rhetoric it might be expected that it would afford new intellectual and social opportunities for women. Humanism's relationship to women was far more ambivalent. In his treatise *On the Family* (1444), Leon Battista Alberti defined a humanist vision of the domestic household, owned by men but run by women:

> the smaller household affairs, I leave to my wife's care . . . it would hardly win us respect if our wife busied herself among the men in the marketplace, out in the public eye. It also seems somewhat demeaning to me to remain shut up in the house among women

when I have manly things to do among men, fellow citizens, and worthy and distinguished foreigners.

The eloquent public man is contrasted with his silent, domestic wife, who remains 'locked up at home'. Her only training is in the running of the household. To ensure its successful maintenance, the husband reveals all its contents to his wife, with just one exception. Only 'my books and records' are kept locked away, and 'these my wife not only could not read, she could not lay hands on them'. Alberti is anxious at the thought 'of bold and forward females who try too hard to know about things outside the house and about the concerns of their husband and of men in general'.

Alberti's attitude influenced humanist responses to elite women who challenged their assigned role and pursued a vocation in humanist learning. They did not completely reject women's pursuit of learning, but were adamant that it should only go so far. In an address written around 1405 Leonardo Bruni, according to Hans Baron the great hero of civic humanism, cautioned that for women to study geometry, arithmetic, and rhetoric was dangerous because 'if a woman throws her arms around while speaking, or if she increases the volume of her speech with greater forcefulness, she will appear threateningly insane and require restraint'. Women could learn cultivation, decorum, and household skills, but formal expertise in applied subjects that could lead to public and professional visibility were frowned upon.

In spite of such hostility, some learned women did attempt to carve out intellectual careers. In *The Book of the City of Ladies* (1404–5) the French writer Christine de Pizan argued that 'those who blame women out of jealousy are those wicked men who have seen and perceived many women of greater intelligence and nobler conduct than they themselves possess'. In the 1430s Isotta Nogarola of Verona responded to attacks on women's loquaciousness by suggesting that, 'rather than women exceeding men in talkativeness, in fact they exceed them in eloquence and virtue'.

However, such forays into publishing and public speaking were regarded as novel events rather than professional activities. In 1438 an anonymous pamphleteer slandered Isotta for attempting to 'speak out'. He conflated her learning with sexual promiscuity, declaiming with a heavy-handed double entendre that 'the woman of fluent tongue is never chaste'. Once a woman crossed the line from accomplished student to orator in the public sphere, the humanist response was to either castigate her for being sexually aggressive, or mystify and trivialize women's intellectual dialogue as amorous exchanges between lovers.

Renaissance humanism did not necessarily create new opportunities for women. It encouraged women's education as a social adornment and an end in itself, not as a means to step out of the household and into the public sphere. Struggling male humanist teachers and students were having enough difficulty carving out their own public and professional positions. The possibility of women achieving such a public profile was clearly threatening, potentially embarrassing, and intolerable. However, the rhetoric of Renaissance humanism extolled the virtues of education and eloquence, and wherever possible women attempted to take advantage of the opportunities afforded by these developments. If women did have a Renaissance, it was often in spite of their male humanist counterparts.

The printing press: a revolution in communication

In the mid-1460s Alberti wrote that he 'approved very warmly of the German inventor who has recently made it possible, by making certain imprints of letters, for three men to make more than two hundred copies of a given original text in one hundred days, since each pressing yields a page in large format'. The invention of movable type in Germany around 1450 was the most important technological and cultural innovation of the Renaissance. Humanism was quick to see the practical possibilities of utilizing a medium of mass reproduction, as Alberti suggests, but the revolutionary effect of print was most pronounced in northern Europe.

The invention of printing emerged from a commercial and technological collaboration in Mainz in the 1450s between Johann Gutenberg, Johann Fust, and Peter Schöffer. Gutenberg was a goldsmith, who adapted his expertise to cast movable metal type for the press. Schöffer was a copyist and calligrapher, who used his skills in copying manuscripts to design, compose, and set the printed text. Fust provided the finance. Printing was a collaborative process, and primarily a commercial business run by entrepreneurs for profit. Drawing on the much earlier eastern inventions of the woodcut and paper, Gutenberg and his team printed a Latin Bible in 1455 and in 1457 issued an edition of the Psalms.

According to Schöffer printing was simply 'the art of writing artificially without reed or pen'. At first, the new medium didn't grasp its own significance. Many early printed books used scribes trained in manuscript illumination to imitate the unique appearance of manuscripts. The opulent decoration of these half-painted, half-printed books suggests that they were regarded as precious commodities in their own right, valued as much for their appearance as their content. Wealthy patrons like Isabella d'Este and Mehmed the Conqueror invested in this type of printed book that sat alongside their more traditional manuscripts.

By 1480 printing presses were successfully established in all the major cities of Germany, France, the Netherlands, England, Spain, Hungary, and Poland. It has been estimated that by 1500 these presses had printed between 6 and 15 million books in 40,000 different editions, more books than had been produced since the fall of the Roman Empire. The figures for the 16th century are even more startling. In England alone 10,000 editions were printed and at least 150 million books were published for a European population of fewer than 80 million people.

The consequence of this massive dissemination of print was a revolution in knowledge and communication that affected society from top to bottom. The speed and quantity with which books were distributed suggests that print cultivated new communities of readers eager to consume the diverse material that rolled off the presses. The accessibility and relatively low cost of printed books also meant that more people than ever before had access to books. Printing was a profitable business. As more people spoke and wrote in the European vernacular languages – German, French, Italian, Spanish, and English – the printing presses increasingly published these languages rather than Latin and Greek, which appealed to a smaller audience. Vernacular languages were gradually standardized. They became the primary means of legal, political, and literary communication in most European states. The mass of printed books in everyday languages contributed to the image of a national community amongst those who shared a common vernacular. This ultimately led individuals to define themselves in relation to a nation rather than a religion or ruler, a situation which had profound consequences for religious authority, with the erosion of the absolute authority of the Catholic Church and the rise of a more secular form of Protestantism.

Printing permeated every area of public and private life. Initially presses issued religious books – Bibles, breviaries, sermons, and catechisms – but gradually more secular books were introduced, like romances, travel narratives, pamphlets, broadsheets, and conduct books advising people on everything from medicine to wifely duties. By the 1530s, printed pamphlets sold for the same price as a loaf of bread, while a copy of the New Testament cost the same as a labourer's daily wage. A culture based on communication through listening, looking, and speaking gradually changed into a culture that interacted through reading and writing. Rather than being focused on courts or churches, a literary culture began to emerge around the semi-autonomous printing press. Its agenda was set by demand and profit rather than religious orthodoxy or political ideology. Printing houses turned intellectual and cultural creativity into a collaborative venture, as printers, merchants, teachers, scribes, translators, artists, and writers all pooled their skills and resources in creating the finished product. One print historian has compared the late 15th-century Venetian printing press of Aldus Manutius to a sweatshop, boarding house, and research institute all in one. Presses like Manutius' created an international community of printers, financiers, and writers, as opportunities for expansion into new markets emerged.

Print also transformed how knowledge itself was understood and transmitted. A manuscript is a unique and unreproducible object. Print, however, with its standard format and type, introduced exact mass reproduction. This meant that two readers separated by distance could discuss and compare identical books, right down to a specific word on a particular page. With the introduction of consistent pagination, indexes, alphabetic ordering, and bibliographies (all unthinkable in manuscripts), knowledge itself was slowly repackaged. Textual scholarship became a cumulative science, as scholars could now gather manuscripts of, say, Aristotle's *Politics* and print a standard authoritative edition based on a comparison of all available copies. This also led to the phenomenon of new and revised editions. Publishers realized the possibility of incorporating discoveries and corrections into the collected works of an author. As well as being intellectually rigorous, this was also commercially very profitable, as individuals could be encouraged to buy a new version of a book they already possessed. Pioneering reference books and encyclopedias on subjects like language and law claimed to reclassify knowledge according to new methodologies of alphabetical and chronological order.

The printing press did not just publish written texts. Part of the revolutionary impact of print was the creation of what William Ivins has called 'the exactly repeatable pictorial statement'. Using woodcuts and then the more sophisticated technique of copperplate engraving, printing made possible the mass diffusion of standardized images of maps, scientific tables and diagrams, architectural plans, medical drawings, cartoons, and religious images. At one end of the social scale visually arresting printed images had a huge impact upon the illiterate, especially when they were used for religious purposes. At the other end, exactly reproducible images revolutionized the study of subjects like geography, astronomy, botany, anatomy, and mathematics. The invention of printing sparked a communications revolution whose impact would be felt for centuries, and which would only be matched by the development of the internet and the revolution in information technology.

The humanist press

Humanists quickly realized the power of the printing press for spreading their own message. The most famous northern European humanist, Desiderius Erasmus of Rotterdam (1466–1536), used the printing press as a way of distributing his own particular brand of humanism, and in the process self-consciously styling himself as the 'Prince of Humanism'. Responding to claims that the early humanists were more interested in classical pagan writers than Christianity, Erasmus embarked on a career of biblical translation and commentary that culminated in his edition of the Greek New Testament with a facing Latin translation (1516). In 'The Ciceronian' (1528) Erasmus countered those Italian humanists that regarded his own brand of northern European humanism as 'barbaric'. He lampooned the purity of the Latinate rhetoric of Ciceronian humanists, arguing that 'the first concern of the Ciceronians should have been to understand the mysteries of the Christian religion, and to turn the pages of the sacred books with as much enthusiasm as Cicero devoted to the writings of philosophers'.

Erasmus endeavoured to fuse his version of classically inspired moral education with a *philosophia Christia* – a philosophy focused on Christ that stressed personal faith. His enormously prolific output embraced translations and commentaries on the classics (including Seneca and Plutarch), collections of Latin proverbs, treatises on language and education, and copious letters to friends, printers, scholars, and rulers across Europe. His most widely read book today is his sardonic *Praise of Folly* (1511). It is a 'biting satire', particularly scathing in its attack upon the corruption and complacency of the church, which is characterized as believing that 'teaching the people is hard work, prayer is boring, tears are weak and womanish, poverty is degrading, and meekness is disgraceful'.

Most of Erasmus's formidable intellectual energy went into constructing an enduring scholarly community and educational method, at the centre of which stood his own printed writings and status as the ultimate 'man of letters'. The printing press was central to Erasmus's manipulation of his intellectual career, right down to the circulation of his own image. In 1526, Dürer agreed to execute an engraving of him. Erasmus and Dürer used this new printing technique to distribute a powerful, commemorative image of the humanist scholar in his study, writing letters and surrounded by his printed books, which as Dürer's Greek inscription suggests, represent Erasmus's lasting fame: 'His works will give a better image of him'.

In 1512 Erasmus published one of his most influential works, *De Copia*, a textbook of exercises in the eloquent expression of Latin. Most famously it contains 200 ways to express the sentiment 'As long as I live, I shall preserve the memory of you.' *De Copia* was written for his friend John Colet, dean of St Paul's School in London. In his dedication to Colet, Erasmus claimed that he wanted 'to make a small literary contribution to the equipment of your school', choosing 'these two new commentaries *De Copia*, inasmuch as the work in question is suitable for boys to read'. Subsequent editions of *De Copia* were dedicated to influential European scholars and patrons, to ensure that the book was used not just in London but also in classrooms across Europe. Erasmus needed to build on the scholarly achievements of 15th-century humanism by using the medium of print to market a whole new way of learning and living.

7. Dürer's portrait of Erasmus, engraved in 1526, established Erasmus's reputation as the great humanist intellectual

Erasmus also appreciated that, as well as reforming education and religion, humanism needed to ingratiate itself with political authority. In 1516 he composed his *Education of a Christian Prince* and dedicated it to the Habsburg prince, the future Emperor Charles V. This was an advice manual for the young prince in how to exercise 'absolute rule over free and willing subjects', and the need for education and advice from those skilled in philosophy and rhetoric. In other words, Erasmus was making a bid for public office as the young prince's personal adviser and public relations guru. Although Charles graciously accepted the manual, no position was forthcoming.

Erasmus's response was to send another copy of *Education of a Christian Prince* to Charles's political rival, King Henry VIII. In his dedication written in 1517 Erasmus praised Henry as a king who managed to 'devote some portion of your time to reading books', which Erasmus argued made Henry 'a better man and a better king'. Erasmus tried to convince Henry that the pursuit of humanism was the best way to run his kingdom, suggesting that it would make him a better person, and provide the skills necessary to achieve his political ends. It is significant that Erasmus felt it appropriate to dedicate the same text to both Charles V and Henry VIII. He presumed that both sovereigns would get the point that he could use his rhetorical skills to construct whatever political argument they required.

The politics of humanism

Erasmus's generation saw the creation of two of the most influential books in the history of political theory and humanism: Niccolò Machiavelli's *The Prince* (1513) and Thomas More's *Utopia* (1516). Today both books are read as timeless classics of how to maintain political power and create ideal societies. They are also highly specific products of both writers' experience of the relationship between humanism and politics in the first half of the 16th century.

Machiavelli's book was written in the wake of the collapse of the Florentine republic in 1512 and the return to power of the Medici family. Machiavelli had served the republic for 14 years before being dismissed and briefly imprisoned by the returning Medici. The intention of *The Prince* was to draw on his political experiences 'to discuss princely government, and to lay down rules about it'. What followed was a devastating account of how rulers should obtain and maintain power. Machiavelli concluded that if his suggestions were 'put into practice skilfully, they will make a new ruler seem very well established, and will quickly make his power more secure'. Machiavelli's background of humanist training and direct political experience produced a series of infamous pronouncements that drew on classical authors as well as contemporary political events. A 'ruler who wishes to maintain his power must be prepared to act immorally'; he should 'be a great feigner and dissembler', ready to 'act treacherously, ruthlessly, or inhumanely, and disregard the precepts of religion' in the interest of retaining political power.

Machiavelli's book was a bid for political employment (or in Machiavelli's case, re-employment). *The Prince* was dedicated to Giuliano de' Medici, the new autocratic ruler of Florence, and was referred to by its author as a 'token of my readiness to serve you'. Machiavelli admitted in his letters 'my desire that these Medici rulers should begin to use me'. *The Prince* was Machiavelli's attempt to offer advice to the Medici on how to hold on to absolute political power. Machiavelli was taking Renaissance humanism to its logical political conclusion in providing his new ruler with the most persuasive and realistic account available of how to retain power. Machiavelli's humanism was prepared to market whatever political ideology was in control, be it autocratic or democratic. The tragedy for Machiavelli was that the Medici were unconvinced by his protestations of loyalty. He never attained high political office again, and *The Prince* remained unprinted at the time of his death in 1527.

Thomas More's *Utopia: Concerning the Best State of a Commonwealth and the New Island of Utopia* was also closely connected to its author's public career. A close friend of Erasmus and gifted student of law and Greek, More translated Lucian and wrote English and Latin poetry. In 1517 he entered Henry VIII's political council and became Lord Chancellor in 1529, writing many of Henry's political and theological tracts in the process. More exemplified Cicero's vision of the cultivated humanist – someone capable of accommodating private philosophical meditation with public oratory and involvement in the civic world of politics and diplomacy.

This delicate balancing act permeates *Utopia*. The book was written in the form of a Latin dialogue between learned men, in direct imitation of Plato's fashionable treatise on an ideal state, the *Republic*. It opens with More himself in Antwerp acting as Henry VIII's diplomatic representative. More's friend introduces him to Raphael Hythloday, an adventurer recently returned from the island of Utopia. Hythloday offers a detailed description of the ideal 'commonwealth' of Utopia, where 'all things are held in common', 'no men are beggars', and divorce, euthanasia, and public health are taken for granted.

Did More believe in his fictionalized vision of an ideal society? There are several reasons for believing that he was rather ambivalent about his Utopia. The word 'utopia' is a pun, a linguistic invention from the Greek, meaning both 'fortunate place' and 'no place'. Hythloday's name also means 'expert in nonsense'. More found many of Utopia's 'laws and customs' 'really absurd', but confessed 'that in the Utopian commonwealth there are many features in our own societies I would like rather than expect to see'. These are heavily qualified endorsements of his imaginary society.

Throughout the book, More refuses to approve or reject the politically contentious issues he discusses, from private property and religious authority to public office and philosophical speculation. This was not because he could not make up his mind: politically, he could not be seen to endorse a particular standpoint. As a skilled political counsellor More had to display his rhetorical skills in justifying often mutually incompatible or contradictory statements and beliefs in the service of the state. Utopia is a canvas upon which he can debate a range of issues relevant to his own particular world. If his analysis was called into question, he could always point out that he argued for the contrary position, or that Utopia was, after all, simply made up: it was nowhere.

Utopia advertises More's ability to eloquently discourse on a range of contentious issues that affected his employer, and upon which he was expected to advise. Unlike Machiavelli, More wrote *Utopia* at the height of his public career and had to be far more circumspect and politically flexible in his thinking. This is why the argument and style of *Utopia* is so paradoxical. The unemployed Machiavelli could offer a much less ambiguous and far more politically realistic account of politics and power in *The Prince*. More's refusal to endorse Henry's divorce was less a principled ethical position than a political miscalculation made on the grounds of religion, leading as it did to More's execution. Both his *Utopia* and Machiavelli's *The Prince* exhibit the political opportunism of the Renaissance humanist.

From Petrarch to More, Renaissance humanism flexibly served whoever it seemed politically expedient to follow. This is why a range of modern political philosophies have claimed that books like *The Prince* and *Utopia* justify their own claims to power and authority. Renaissance humanism continues to exercise a powerful influence upon the modern humanities, yet as this chapter has argued, humanism is not the idealized celebration of humaneness that it often claimed to be, but has a hard core of pragmatism. The legacy of Renaissance humanism is far more ambivalent than many have been led to believe, partly because its rhetoric remains so seductive.

Chapter 3
Church and state

In 1435 the humanist scholar Lorenzo Valla arrived in Naples to offer his services to its future king, Alfonso of Aragon. At the time Alfonso was locked in a political struggle with Pope Eugenius IV over possession of Naples. Valla went to work on a text of direct political relevance to his new paymaster: the *Donation of Constantine*. The *Donation* was one of the founding documents of the Roman Catholic Church. It purported to be a grant issued in the 4th century by the Emperor Constantine that awarded sweeping imperial and territorial powers to the papacy. It was one of the most powerful and convincing justifications of papal claims to worldly authority. Lorenzo Valla exposed the *Donation* as a fake. Using his humanist skills in rhetoric, philosophy, and philology, he demonstrated that its historical anachronisms, philological errors, and contradictions in logic revealed that the *Donation* was an 8th-century forgery.

The deftness of Valla's textual analysis was matched by his scathing attack upon the Roman Church and its pontiffs, who had either 'not known that the *Donation of Constantine* is spurious and forged, or else they forged it'. He accused them of 'dishonouring the Christian religion, confounding everything with murders, disasters and crimes'. Valla ridiculed the inaccurate and anachronistic Latin of the *Donation*, before again posing the rhetorical question 'can we justify the principle of papal power when we perceive it to be the cause of such great crimes and of such great and varied evils?' This rhetorically elegant invective concluded with an attack upon the imperial pretensions of the pope, who, 'so that he may recover the other parts of the *Donation*, money wickedly stolen from good people he spends more wickedly'. Alfonso was delighted with Valla's demolition of the *Donation* and used its arguments in his ultimately successful attempt to secure the kingdom of Naples despite concerted papal opposition.

The story of Valla's revelation represents a new development in the relations between Renaissance religion, politics, and learning. The rise of political organizations like the sovereign state created the need for new intellectual and administrative skills to organize political structures and successfully challenge the authority of institutions like the church. The fact that Pope Martin V subsequently employed Valla as a papal secretary may seem surprising in the light of his exposure of the *Donation*. However, it reveals the church's attitude towards such scholars (better the devil you know). It also shows how politically strategic humanists like Valla were prepared to be when new opportunities beckoned.

This story helps us to understand the complex interrelation of the religion and politics of the Renaissance. Between 1400 and 1600 religious belief was an integral part of everyday life. It was also impossible to separate religion from the practice of political authority, the world of international finance, and the achievements of art and learning. As the Catholic Church struggled to assert its temporal and spiritual power throughout this period, it faced perpetual conflict, dissent, and division. This culminated in the Reformation that swept through 16th-century northern Europe, creating the greatest crisis in the history of the Roman Church. The Catholic Counter-Reformation of the mid-16th century transformed the Church forever and, combined with the Protestant Reformation led by Martin Luther, established the general shape of Christianity as it exists today. The Reformation also raised complex questions concerning Christianity's relationship with the other two great religions of the book, Judaism and Islam, both of which asserted their theological superiority over Christianity, and which in the case of Islam was quick to exploit the schisms of the 16th-century Christian church. Religion in the Renaissance was in perpetual crisis. Doubt, anxiety, and inward contemplation remain cornerstones of modern thinking and subjectivity, and their origins can be traced back to the religious ferment of the period 1400–1600.

The other development that transformed religious authority within this period was the rise of new forms of political authority. From the late 15th century political organizations increasingly came to control the everyday lives of many people. The wealth and administrative innovation that accompanied the uneven commercial and urban expansion of the 15th century created the conditions for significant political upheaval and expansion. Italian cities like Florence and Venice experimented with republican governments, while the courts of Milan, Naples, Urbino, and Ferrara ruled as petty principalities. In the north, the peace and prosperity following the Hundred Years War concentrated wealth and power in France and the Low Countries, spawning the great Habsburg Empire. To the east, the Ottoman Empire provided a model of global imperial power against which all others must compete. By the middle of the 16th century, Europe was in the control of a series of sovereign states and empires – France, Portugal, Spain, and the Ottomans. Their rise was in inverse proportion to the worldly power of the church.

By the beginning of the 15th century, the Catholic Church was in crisis. The word 'Catholic' came from the Greek word for 'universal', but by 1400 the church looked anything but universal. The church had already experienced division with its separation into the Western, Roman Church and the Eastern, Orthodox Church based in Constantinople in 1054. Over the following three centuries the Western Church battled to assert its theological and imperial authority in the face of opposition from inside and outside. The pope claimed by biblical authority that, as Christ's representative on earth, he held political sway over worldly issues.

Throughout the 14th century the papacy was split between rival claimants in Rome and Avignon in France. The Papal Schism allowed dissident cardinals from both sides to propose the conciliar theory of church governance. This led church councils to impose their collective authority over schismatic popes. In 1414 the church fathers convened the Council of Constance to put an end to the schism. The Council ruled that 'all men, of every rank and condition, including the pope himself, are bound to obey it in matters concerning the Faith, the abolition of the schism, and the reformation of the Church of God'. This allowed the Council to appoint Martin V as the first uncontested Roman pope for nearly a century.

An orthodox marriage

The Council of Constance unintentionally increased the autocratic power of the papacy. Both Pope Martin V and his successor, Eugenius IV, consolidated their authority by embarking on ambitious plans to rebuild Rome and unite with the Eastern Orthodox Church. In 1437 Eugenius convened the Council of Florence to discuss the unification of the Eastern Orthodox and Western Roman Churches and deflect the Council's attempts to reduce papal authority. In February 1438 the Byzantine Emperor John VIII Paleologus arrived in Florence with a retinue of 700 Greeks and the head of the Orthodox Church, the Patriarch Joseph II. As well as the Greek delegation, deputations arrived from Trebizond, Russia, Armenia, Cairo, and Ethiopia. As with many Renaissance transactions ostensibly concerned with religion, this momentous official meeting between east and west had profound political and cultural implications. John VIII proposed a union between the eastern and western branches of Christendom as the only realistic way to prevent the collapse of the Byzantine Empire and the capture of Constantinople in the face of the rise of the Ottoman Empire. The pope was eager to unify the two churches as a way of extending his own political power throughout Italy.

Away from official council business, delegates enthusiastically explored each other's intellectual and cultural achievements. The Greeks admired the architectural achievements of Brunelleschi, the sculpture of Donatello, and the frescos of Masaccio and Fra Angelico. The Florentines marvelled at the extraordinary collection of classical books that John VIII and his scholarly retinue had brought with them from Constantinople. These included manuscripts of Plato, Aristotle, Plutarch, Euclid, and Ptolemy and other classical texts which were 'not accessible here' in Italy according to one envious scholar. The Egyptian delegation presented the pope with a 10th-century Arabic manuscript of the Gospels, and the Armenian delegation left behind 13th-century illuminated manuscripts on the Armenian Church that reflected its mixed Mongol, Christian, and Islamic heritage. The Ethiopian delegation also circulated 15th-century Psalters written in Ethiopic and used in churches throughout north-east Africa.

Twenty years after the council, Benozzo Gozzoli completed his frescos in the Palazzo Medici that celebrated the Medici role in bringing together the Eastern and Western Churches. In Gozzoli's frescos John VIII, Joseph II, and Lorenzo de' Medici have become the three Magi. For political reasons Lorenzo's forebear, Cosimo de' Medici, had bankrolled the entire Council. The Medici had been negotiating commercial access to Constantinople throughout the 1430s, but an agreement was only reached in August 1439 as a token of John VIII's thanks for Cosimo's lavish hospitality throughout the Council of Florence. Cosimo's pious act of financial sacrifice for the good of the church was actually a clever sleight of hand. Eugenius remained even more financially indebted to the Medici, and Gozzoli's frescos make it clear that the family regarded their involvement in unifying the two churches as even more important than the mediation of the pope.

8. Benozzo Gozzoli's fresco *The Adoration of the Magi*: an artistic attempt by the Medici to take the credit for uniting the Eastern and Western Churches

On 6 July 1439 the Decree of Union was finally signed between the two churches. It rejoiced that 'the wall which separated the Eastern Church and the Western Church has been destroyed, and peace and concord have returned'. The rejoicing was short-lived. Back in Constantinople, the union was rejected by the populace, stirred up by members of the Eastern Church, while the Italian states demonstrated their reluctance by consistently refusing to provide military aid to assist the Byzantines in their struggle against the Ottomans. With the fall of Constantinople to Mehmed II in May 1453, the union came to a bloody and ignominious end.

The Council of Florence was a defining moment of the Renaissance. As a religious summit, it was a failure, crushing the papacy's hopes for the consolidation of its own imperial power through unification with the Eastern Church. As a political and cultural event, it was a triumph. It allowed the Italian states to challenge the authority of a weakened papacy, and strengthen commercial relations to the east. Ruling families cleverly manipulated their own role in the Council, through sumptuous art objects like Gozzoli's frescos that claimed Medici pre-eminence in bringing about the Decree of Union. Culturally, the transmission of classical texts, ideas, and art objects from east to west that took place at the Council was to have a decisive effect on the art and scholarship of late 15th-century Italy.

The masses

What of the everyday reality of religious observance for the millions of people across Europe who regularly attended church and identified themselves as Christians? It would be idealistic to believe that debates about papal authority and textual exegesis had much impact upon many of these people. The church was part of the fabric of everyday life for most individuals, and this meant that the distinction between the sacred and the profane often became blurred. Churches were used for festivals, political meetings, eating, horse-trading, and even storing merchants' goods and valuables. The clergy were everywhere. By 1550 out of a population of 60,000, Florence boasted over 5,000 clergymen. Poorly educated and badly paid, they were often to be found working as masons, horse dealers, and cattle traders, keeping lovers and children, and carrying weapons.

In theory, the Catholic Church acted as the earthly manifestation of Christ's incarnation. It mediated between God and the individual, and was exclusively responsible for dispensing God's grace through the sacraments – baptism, confirmation, the Eucharist, penance, ordination, marriage, and extreme unction. According to the theory of transubstantiation, the priest possessed the miraculous (arguably magical) power of transforming the bread and wine of the Eucharist into the real body and blood of Christ. Without the intercession of the church and the priest, the individual had no direct contact with God. In the performance of the sacraments, the priest alone brought God into direct touch with the laity. It was this mediating role which made the church such a powerful institution.

In practice, the most enthusiastic public interest in religious observance revolved around what one historian has called a passionate 'appetite for the divine'. The 'miracles' of the sacraments were often interpreted as magical acts, and led to the adoption of a range of popular practices, from the fervent worship of relics, saints, and images to the superstitious use of holy water, the Eucharist, and holy oil. Although such magical practices went against religious orthodoxy, the church often turned a blind eye to such transgressions, eager to sustain the mystical power of the church and its authority.

For most people, the church provided a ritual method of living day to day, rather than a set of rigid theological beliefs. The sacraments of baptism, confirmation, marriage, and extreme unction provided rites of passage through crucial moments in an individual's life. As a consequence, many people only went to church once or twice a year, and court records reveal remarkably low attendances, as well as profound ignorance on basic points of religion. One English preacher told the story of a shepherd who when asked about the Father, Son, and Holy Ghost replied, 'The father and the son I know well for I tend their sheep, but I know not the third fellow; there is none of that name in our village.' At best, this attitude represented religious ignorance and indifference; at worst, it suggested heresy and unbelief, which took various forms throughout the Renaissance period and beyond.

In the 1440s the bishop of Tournai, Jean Chevrot, was so concerned at the poor attendance and observation of the sacraments that he commissioned Roger van der Weyden to paint an altarpiece that would educate people in the ritual significance of the sacraments, simply entitled the *Seven Sacraments*. The left panel of van der Weyden's triptych shows baptism, confirmation, and confession, while the right panel shows ordination, marriage, and extreme unction. The central panel is reserved for the most important sacrament, the Eucharist, which takes place behind the revelation of Christ. To avoid any confusion, angels helpfully float above each sacrament, holding banners with explanatory verses. By using contemporary figures, architecture, and clothing, van der Weyden's triptych employs a typically Renaissance technique of 'vulgarization', where the mysteries of the church are set against modern settings that encourage the congregation's close identification with the painted image. The quiet intensity of the scene was also noticeably devoid of the jostling, hawking, joking, spitting, swearing, knitting, begging, sleeping, and even gun-firing that were a daily feature of church life.

9. Roger van der Weyden's altarpiece the *Seven Sacraments* tries to educate a 15th-century congregation about the sacraments

Building the Reformation

When Pope Martin V ended the factional schism and returned to Rome in 1420, 'he found it so dilapidated and deserted that it hardly bore any resemblance to a city', never mind the capital of both the former Roman Empire and the future Catholic Empire. The response of Martin and his successors was to begin an ambitious building programme that would celebrate the glory of the newly centralized Roman Church. It would also turn the city into a building site for the following 150 years. In the words of Pope Nicholas V, the laity would find their 'belief continually confirmed and daily corroborated by great buildings' that were 'seemingly made by the hand of God'. Alberti, Fra Angelico, Bramante, Michelangelo, Raphael, and Botticelli were just some of the artists who came to be associated with the rebuilding of the city.

The biggest problem that successive popes faced was the renovation of the crumbling basilica of St Peter's, built on the saint's tomb by Constantine in the mid-4th century. As has already been said, Rome was already competing with Constantinople as imperial capital of the Christian world. The competition became even fiercer once that city fell to Sultan Mehmed in 1453. Rome and its popes did not want to be outshone by Istanbul and its sultans. In April 1506 Pope Julius II laid the cornerstone for the new St Peter's, having appointed Bramante as its architect. The foundation medal cast by Caradosso shows how closely Bramante's original design was modelled on Hagia Sophia. Subsequent revisions by Raphael, Sangallo, and Michelangelo throughout the 16th century led to the completion of St Peter's as it looks today.

Ironically it was the cost of completing this monumental celebration of papal authority that started a protest that would ultimately challenge the core of the Catholic Church, and transform the social and political landscape of Europe forever. In 1510, four

10. Caradosso's medal commemorates the beginning of work on
St Peter's in 1506, and shows that the early designs borrowed from
Byzantine and Ottoman architecture

years after work began on St Peter's, and as Michelangelo laboured
on his frescos for the ceiling of the Sistine Chapel, the German
monk Martin Luther arrived in Rome. His disillusionment with the
corruption and conspicuous consumption he witnessed provided
the inspiration for the beginning of his attack upon the abuses of
the Catholic Church – the circulation of his 95 theses against
indulgences in October 1517. In March of that year, the pope had
issued an indulgence to finance the building of St Peter's. An
indulgence was a papal document that granted the buyer remission
from the need to do penance for his sins. So eager was the church to
finance the rebuilding of Rome that indulgences were even sold to

individuals to cover uncommitted future sins. The church had created a trade in salvation that allowed the individual to buy and sell deliverance. Luther was outraged. He wrote to the archbishop of Mainz, complaining:

> Papal indulgences for the building of St Peter's are circulating under your most distinguished name ... I grieve over the wholly false impressions which the people have conceived from them; to wit – the unhappy souls believe that if they have purchased letters of indulgence they are sure of their salvation.

Luther repeated his protest in the 95 theses famously circulated throughout the town of Wittenberg. 'Why does not the pope', wrote Luther, 'whose wealth is to-day greater than the riches of the richest, build just this one church of St Peter with his own money, rather than with the money of poor believers?' The first shot of the European Reformation had been fired.

Faith wars

Like the term 'Renaissance', 'Reformation' is a retrospective term applied to the consequences of Luther's ideas. Luther did indeed set out with the idea of reforming the church, but reformation quickly turned into revolution. Luther's protest against indulgences soon crystallized into a systematic rejection of every religious assumption upon which the Catholic Church rested. Luther argued that the individual possessed a direct relationship with God, and could not rely on the mediation of priests, saints, or indulgences to grant salvation; the individual could only maintain absolute faith in the grace of an inscrutable but ultimately merciful God in the hope of being saved. There was nothing weak and evil individuals could do in the face of God, but hold on to faith, the ultimate gift from God. Worldly attempts to change the state of one's soul through indulgences and penances were meaningless. As Luther himself concluded, 'A Christian has all that he needs in faith and needs no works to justify him.'

The implication of all this for the Catholic Church was profound. Having abandoned papal mediation between God and the individual, at a stroke Luther rejected the authority of both pope and priest. The theatre and paraphernalia of church ritual were rejected, as was the distinction between clergy and laity. Luther also condemned all but two of the sacraments. He argued that God gave faith directly to the individual, and did not appear through intermediaries, be they priests or sacramental rituals.

The impact of Luther's ideas was complex but immediate. As he refined and expanded his position in response to increasingly alarmed Catholic reaction, 'Lutheranism' spread throughout northern Europe with astonishing speed and profound consequences way beyond Luther's control. By the time of his death in 1546, councils with reformed church tendencies controlled Wittenberg, Nuremberg, Strasbourg, Zurich, Berne, and Basle. Lutheranism found fertile ground amongst a predominantly civic, urban laity disaffected with Catholicism. Monastic orders and traditional worship were abolished, church property was smashed or confiscated, and religious images were destroyed in iconoclastic riots. In their place came new sites and methods of worship, and idealistic experiments in social and political reform. In 1524 the German peasants rose up, seeking justification for their grievances in Luther's teachings. He contemptuously condemned the 'poisonous, hurtful' rebellion, revealing the limits of his radicalism when it came to more worldly matters.

Luther was also unable to control the intellectual impact of many of his arguments. By the 1540s Geneva was under the control of the theology of John Calvin, who argued that man was powerless to influence divine predestination. For Calvin, God had always already decided who would be damned and who saved. In England, Henry VIII's political decision to split from Rome in 1533 led ultimately to the excommunication of Henry's daughter, Queen Elizabeth I, for what was by then called her 'Protestantism'.

Printing the Word

Humanism and printing lay at the heart of the rise and spread of Luther's ideas. Luther and his followers utilized humanist training in philology, rhetoric, and translation to produce a theology based on 'the Word' and 'Scripture alone'. What united reformers like Luther and humanists including Erasmus was a commitment to close biblical interpretation, or exegesis, which challenged the perceived ignorance and superstition of earlier scholastic thinking. Luther could match the finest papal scholarship, boasting in his discussion *On Translating* (1530) that 'I can do their dialectics and philosophy better than all of them put together'. He parted company with humanism when he realized the limits of its commitment to change, telling Erasmus that 'it matters little to you what anyone believes anywhere, as long as the peace of the world is undisturbed'. However, humanism had already supplied Lutheranism with the intellectual tools to transform religion. It had also provided Luther with the object that would transmit his new ideas all over Europe: the printing press.

Writing on the spread of his ideas in 1522, Luther claimed 'I did nothing; the Word did everything'. He was right. It was the medium of print that circulated 'the Word'. Earlier challengers to papal authority had little ability to circulate their ideas to a wider audience, but the technology of the printing press allowed Luther to disseminate his ideas in thousands of printed books, broadsides, and pamphlets. The German states were also the perfect location from which to spread a religious revolution, being at the geographical and technological heart of Europe. By 1520 62 German cities possessed printing presses, and between 1517 and 1524 the publication of printed books in these cities increased sevenfold. One of the reasons for this increased output was Luther himself. He soon realized the radical potential of the printing press, calling it 'God's highest and extremest act of grace, whereby the business of the Gospel is driven forward'. Between 1517 and 1520 Luther wrote over 30 tracts, with more than 300,000 copies printed. One admiring friend claimed that, 'Luther is the man who can keep two printers busy, each working two presses'. Luther also realized the power of spreading his Word in the vernacular, rather than the elite church language of Latin. By 1575 his printed German translation of the Bible had sold an estimated 100,000 copies. It has been further estimated that his works represented one third of all German-language books sold between 1518 and 1525. By 1530, Luther had become the first best-selling author in the short history of print.

Lutheranism emerged from a world in which the commercial, financial, and political centre of gravity had gradually shifted northwards. By the beginning of the 16th century Antwerp was overtaking Venice as the commercial capital of Europe, and the German states that gave birth to Lutheranism were also forging new political identities that would create a recognizably modern map of Europe by the end of the century. By 1519 Charles V of the House of Habsburg added Austria to his dynastic inheritance of Spain, Naples, the Netherlands, and the New World. His election to the title of Holy Roman Emperor initiated a monumental political power struggle throughout Europe that saw Charles, King Francis I, and Henry VIII, as well as John III of Portugal and Sultan Süleyman, vie for territorial and political control, with the city states of Italy reduced to the status of helpless bargaining counters. The seeds of nationalist revolt were also beginning to stir in northern Europe, and to the east Charles faced the overwhelming imperial power of Süleyman, who conquered Belgrade in 1521 and by 1529 was laying siege to Vienna. The rise of Lutheranism only compounded Charles's difficulties.

Charles was keen not to alienate his German allies by excommunicating one of its monks. However, following Luther's personal promise to the emperor himself that 'I cannot and I will not retract anything, since it is neither safe nor right to go against conscience', Charles condemned him as 'a notorious heretic'. The German states resisted papal calls for the destruction of

'Protestantism', as it was called from 1529 when a group of German princes 'protested' against calls for the condemnation of Lutheranism. Charles was distracted by the administration of his overseas possessions as well as being faced with the spectre of Sultan Süleyman the Magnificent beating at the door of his own empire.

By 1529 Süleyman's empire stretched across North Africa, the Mediterranean, and most of eastern Europe, and was in league with Charles's enemy, Francis I. While the Ottomans continued to confront Charles as political equals, their faith also became an issue in the increasingly polarized religious atmosphere of the 1520s. Like Francis, Luther and his followers considered the possibility of a strategic alliance with the Ottomans as a bulwark against Charles's Habsburg Empire. Luther studied the Koran, and participated in the publication of several German texts on Islam. Following the calls of various Lutheran pamphleteers to 'seek the enemy in Italy, not in the East!' he cautiously argued that 'if we must have any Turkish war, we ought to begin with ourselves'. This suggested that the Ottoman threat was sent by God to plague the Catholic emperor and pope. Süleyman also realized how Lutheranism could play into Ottoman hands by distracting the Habsburgs from concentrating on the military threat from the east. Both Islam and Protestantism were aware that theologically their belief in the power of the book and opposition to idolatry made a political rapprochement a distinct possibility in the volatile years of the mid-16th century.

Charles V was far less ideologically flexible. His dynastic heritage was based on the expulsion of both the Jews and the Moors from Spain in 1492. He and his advisers soon became convinced that Luther and Süleyman represented two sides of the same coin, both 'heretics' that must be exterminated. In 1523 the papal nuncio based in Nuremberg wrote that 'we are occupied with the negotiations for the general war against the Turk, and for that particular war against that nefarious Martin Luther, who is a greater evil to Christendom than the Turk'. In 1530 Cardinal

Campeggio wrote to Charles that Luther's 'diabolical and heretical opinions . . . shall be castigated and punished according to the rule and practice observed in Spain with regard to the Moors'.

As the zeal for religious reformation collided with increasingly ambitious claims to global political authority, religious intolerance intensified. Jewish communities had lived throughout Europe for centuries, in spite of their official expulsion from England in 1290 and Spain in 1492. However, in such a period of polarized religious positions, the Jews soon found themselves persecuted by both Catholics and Protestants, accused of crimes that ranged from poisoning wells to murdering Christian babies. In 1555 Pope Paul IV issued a papal bull attacking the Jewish faith, claiming that the church only 'tolerates Jews in order that they may bear witness to true Christian faith'. Jews could convert to Catholicism, otherwise they were forbidden to own property, and were confined to ghettos where they were required to wear a yellow badge as a sign of infamy. Protestantism was hardly any more tolerant. In 1514 Luther claimed that 'the Jews will always curse and blaspheme God and his King Christ'. He later claimed, 'I would rather have the Turks for enemies than the Spaniards for protectors: for barbarous tyrants as they are, most of the Spaniards are half Moors, half Jews, fellows who believe nothing at all.' The Spanish Catholics in turn saw Protestants as heretics comparable to Muslims and Jews. As Catholicism responded to the threat of Lutheranism, and Protestantism tried to define itself in clear theological distinction to other religions, both increasingly attacked the two religions of the book that did not subscribe to the belief that Jesus was the Son of God.

These conflicts also changed the shape of Renaissance art. As the papacy in Rome sensed the erosion of its political power, it responded with even more lavish displays of art and architecture in an attempt to reaffirm its authority. The strain showed in the art of Michelangelo and Raphael. Michelangelo's frescos of scenes from Genesis that decorate the Sistine Chapel, commissioned by Pope

Julius II, offer a comprehensive view of creation based on the teachings of Rome. The graceful dynamism of the scenes and the powerful, straining musculature of its characters also idealize the power and potential wrath of the Roman Church if questioned. This tension is also detectable in Raphael's frescos for the Vatican's Salon of Constantine. They tell the story of the life of the Emperor Constantine, and the shift in church power from the east (Constantine's imperial seat of Constantinople) to the west (St Peter's in Rome).

The final scene in the fresco cycle, entitled the *Donation of Constantine*, shows the Emperor Constantine handing over his worldly and imperial power to the pope, wearing a tiara that demonstrates both his spiritual and worldly power. Just months after work began on the Constantine Salon, Luther wrote,

> I have at hand Lorenzo Valla's proof that the Donation of Constantine is a forgery. Good heavens, what darkness and wickedness is at Rome. You wonder at the judgement of God that such unauthentic, crass, impudent lies not only lived, but prevailed for so many centuries.

Valla's treatise on the Donation had been printed for the first time in Germany in 1517 as part of the growing attack upon the Roman Church. The frescos in the Salon of Constantine, with their towering popes, warring factions, and dramatic scenes of papal authority are aggressive, mannered, and anxious responses to religious and political change. The printed 'word' from the north was triumphing over the towering monuments and glorious frescos of the south.

The empire strikes back

The Roman Church soon realized that triumphant art was no answer to the questions posed by the dramatic rise of northern European Protestantism. In 1545 Pope Paul III convened the

11. The fresco the *Donation of Constantine* was painted in the Vatican by Raphael's workshop between 1523 and 1524. Religious conflict shapes its imperial content and mannered, aggressive style

Council of Trent to reform the church and refute Lutheranism. Over the next 18 years the council drafted decrees that formed the basis of the Catholic Counter-Reformation. The Council reaffirmed the sanctity of the seven sacraments, transubstantiation, purgatory, and papal authority. It endorsed the veneration of saints, relics, and the purchase of indulgences, while also reforming the abuses that had so angered Luther. Religious orders were reformed, seminaries were established for the training of priests, and bishops were expected to take a more proactive approach to the administration of their dioceses. The Council endorsed the creation in 1540 of the Society of Jesus (better known as the Jesuit order), led by the Spaniard Ignatius Loyola, and the establishment in 1542 of the Roman Inquisition that hunted down heretics and reformers.

The Council also turned its attention to the most pernicious carrier of the Protestant Reformation – the printed book. In 1563 it issued an index of forbidden books deemed 'heretical', declaring 'if anyone should read or possess books by heretics or writings by any author condemned and prohibited by reason of heresy or suspicion of false teaching, he incurs immediately the sentence of excommunication'. The Index forbade thousands of books, starting with the works of Luther, Zwingli, and Calvin, but also including the works of Machiavelli and selected writings of Erasmus. Trent implicitly conceded the power of the printed book (partly through the funding of Catholic printing presses to publish orthodox texts), but at the cost of establishing one of the first modern attempts at mass censorship.

The Council of Trent's zealous mix of reform, piety, militancy, and repression was remarkably successful. It has been calculated that by the end of the 16th century nearly a third of the laity lost to Rome had returned to the fold as a result of the Counter-Reformation. However, its attitude towards religious observance, books, and even images further polarized the religious landscape of the later 16th century. Trent underlined the widening gulf between the ideology of Protestantism and Catholicism, and in the process paved the way for the religious wars of the latter half of the century that would redefine the shape of Europe.

By 1600, Europe had changed beyond all recognition from the ill-defined collection of city states and principalities that made little reference to the entity of 'Europa' in 1400. Nation states and emerging global empires set the political agenda, and the fluidity of religious encounters and exchanges between east and west had hardened into the programmatic belief systems of Catholicism, Protestantism, and Islam. This signalled the birth of the modern institution of the state and the concomitant rise of nationalism. The great imperial powers of Europe would go on to claim most of the newly discovered globe over the next three centuries. But the legacy of the period was also a series of seemingly irresolvable religious and political conflicts in regions as diverse as Ireland, the Balkans, and the Middle East, whose origins lay in the collision of church and state that first took place in the Renaissance.

4
Brave new worlds

In 1482 a printing press in the German town of Ulm published a new edition of Ptolemy's *Geography*. Its world map captured what the world looked like to Europe's 15th-century ruling elite. Ptolemy wrote his *Geography* in Alexandria in the 2nd century AD. Arabic scholars had preserved and revised the text prior to its translation into Latin by the end of the 14th century. Medieval Christian geography had been limited to schematic maps, known as *mappae mundi*, which were religious symbols of the Christian understanding of creation. They placed Jerusalem at their centre, with little or no attempt to understand or represent the wider world. Ptolemy's *Geography* transformed 15th-century perceptions of the shape and size of the earth. His text listed and described over 8,000 places, as well as explaining how to draw regional and world maps. The geometrical grid of latitude and longitude that Ptolemy threw across the known world provided the template used by the 15th- and 16th-century voyages of trade and discovery, which began to shape today's modern image of the globe, and which form the basis of this chapter.

For a late 15th-century ruler or merchant, the Ulm version of Ptolemy provided a reasonably accurate representation of the world of the time. 'Europa' and the Mediterranean, 'Affrica' and 'Asia' are all recognizable. What seems erroneous to us today is the omission of the Americas, Australasia, the Pacific, the bulk of the Atlantic

12. Ptolemy's world map from one of the new printed editions of his classical text *Geography*, published in Ulm in 1482

Ocean, and the southern tip of Africa (without which the Indian Ocean is represented as a giant lake). Ptolemy's world centred on the eastern Mediterranean and central Asia, on cities like Constantinople, Baghdad, and Alexandria. These locations represented the predominant international reality of educated people from the 2nd century AD right down to the close of the 15th century.

The *Geography* was owned by princes, clerics, scholars, and merchants eager to display their own awareness of geography and travel through possession of expensive manuscript copies of Ptolemy. However, working maps that survive from the 14th century show the mixed cultural traditions that shaped the Renaissance world. The anonymous Maghreb chart, dated around 1330, is a practical example of the so-called 'portolan' charts used by merchants and navigators to move across the Mediterranean. The 'rhumb' lines that criss-cross the map aid compass bearings and allow navigators to sail reasonably accurate courses. Produced in either Granada or Morocco, it demonstrates the circulation of geographical knowledge, navigation skills, and trade between Christian and Muslim communities. Of its 202 place names, 48 are of Arabic origin, the rest Catalan, Hispanic, or Italian. Based on the expertise of Arab, Jewish, and Christian navigators and scholars, it was practical charts such as these that enabled the first tentative seaborne voyages beyond the bounds of Europe.

Rounding the Cape

In 1415 the Portuguese captured the Muslim city of Ceuta in Morocco. The victory gave Portugal a springboard for expansion down the West African coast. Taking advantage of its geographical location facing out into the Atlantic, the Portuguese crown sought to break into the trans-Saharan trade routes, circumventing the need to pay crippling tariffs that burdened overland and seaborne trade routes via North Africa back into southern Europe. As the

13. This sea chart, or 'portolan', the 'Maghreb chart', was drawn in North Africa around 1330 and shows how shared knowledge shaped Mediterranean navigation

Portuguese crown claimed Madeira (1420), the Azores (1439), and the Cape Verde Islands (1460s), the trade in basic materials like timber, sugar, fish, and wheat became more important than the glamorous search for gold. This led to a redefinition of the aims of seaborne discovery and settlement on the part of the Portuguese crown.

Once they had settled the Azores, the Portuguese were sailing south into uncharted territories, or what was labelled on Ptolemy's map 'Terra Incognita'. Having reached the limit of Mediterranean traditions of navigation and map-making, the Portuguese employed the services of Jewish scholars to develop solar tables, star charts, astrolabes, quadrants, and cross staffs to calculate latitude according to the position of the sun, moon, and stars. By the 1480s these scientific developments were so successful that the Portuguese had rounded Sierra Leone and established trading posts (or *feitoria*) along the Guinea coast.

The commercial encounters that stemmed from these developments had a noticeable impact upon the culture and economy of communities in West Africa, Portugal, and the rest of mainland Europe. The mingling of people led to the creation of autonomous mixed-race communities in West Africa, referred to as *lançados*. Copper, horses, and cloth were also traded for gold, pepper, ivory, and ebony. By the end of the 15th century the gold shipped back to Lisbon allowed Portugal to issue its first national gold coin, the *crusado*, and embark on an ambitious public building programme that fused classical, Mughal, and Persian motifs, and which even today can be seen as far afield as Lisbon, Goa, and Macau.

In December 1488 Bartolomeu Diaz returned to Lisbon to announce that he had sailed around the southernmost tip of Africa. A contemporary Portuguese geographer recorded that Diaz realized 'that the coast here turned northwards and north-eastwards towards Ethiopia under Egypt and on to the Gulf of Arabia, giving great hope of the discovery of India'. As a result Diaz 'called it the "Cape of Good Hope"'. The news rendered printed maps still reproducing Ptolemy's view of the world increasingly obsolete. From now on, European voyagers really were sailing into 'terra incognita', a whole New World where they could no longer rely on classical authority.

East is east

One observer who was particularly impressed by these discoveries was the Genoese navigator Christopher Columbus, who was present at the Portuguese court when Diaz returned with news of his circumnavigation of the Cape. It was Columbus's observation of the practical achievements of the Portuguese navigators and his immersion in classical geography that led him to make a fateful decision. Columbus accepted Ptolemy and Marco Polo's massive overestimation of the size of Asia. But he also realized that, if Ptolemy's estimate of the circumference of the world were correct, then a voyage to Asia that sailed westwards from Europe would be much shorter than the south-eastern route followed by the Portuguese. Columbus calculated that the westward distance between Japan and the Azores was 3,000 miles. It was in fact over 10,000 miles. Ptolemy's calculations on both the size of Asia and the globe were wrong. If Columbus had known this, he might never have embarked on his voyage in 1492.

Columbus first proposed the idea to the Portuguese court in 1485, but his plan was rejected because of Lisbon's success in pursuing the sea route to the east via southern Africa. So Columbus took his proposal to the Castilian crown. Castile was in financial trouble due to its ongoing struggle against the Iberian Muslims. The possibility of cornering the market in spices and gold from the east was too good to miss, and they offered Columbus financial backing. On 2 August 1492, Columbus finally departed on his first voyage from Palos in southern Spain, in command of 90 men in three ships.

After nearly two months sailing westwards across the Atlantic, on Thursday, 10 October, Columbus sighted the Bahamas, where he landed and encountered locals, who 'were all very well built, with very handsome bodies and very good faces', and were also perceived to be 'good servants and of quick intelligence'. Columbus was impatient 'to leave for another very large island, which I believe must be Cipangu [Japan], according to the signs which these Indians whom I have with me make; they call it "Colba"'. Columbus was convinced that he was on the verge of reaching Japan. 'Colba' turned out to be Cuba. He skirted the coast of Cuba and Haiti, before wrecking his flagship and heading home with small traces of gold and several kidnapped 'Indians'.

Columbus's return to Europe caused a diplomatic storm. This was not because he had discovered a 'New World' – he still clung to the belief that he had reached the east by sailing west. Portugal objected that the Castilian-backed expedition broke the terms of an earlier agreement that guaranteed the Portuguese monopoly on all discoveries 'beyond Guinea'. But the ambiguity of this phrase, and the intercession of a sympathetic Spanish pope, granted the new discoveries to Castile under the terms of the Treaty of Tordesillas (1494). The treaty also stipulated that a map be drawn up with a line of partition defining the relative spheres of interest of the two crowns. The delegates agreed that 'a boundary or straight line be determined and drawn' running down the Atlantic, 'at a distance of three hundred and seventy leagues west of the Cape Verde Islands'. Everything to the west of this line belonged to Castile, everything to the east (and south) belonged to Portugal. Castile got what it believed was a new route to the east, while the Portuguese protected their African possessions and passage to the east via the Cape of Good Hope.

The jewel in the crown

Columbus's initial 'discovery' of America was seen as a failure. He appeared to have discovered a new territorial obstacle blocking the path to a shorter, commercially lucrative route to the east. The Portuguese, delayed in their attempt to capitalize on Diaz's discovery of the Cape by Columbus's voyage and the subsequent diplomatic dispute, dispatched another expedition round the Cape with the explicit aim of reaching India. In July 1497 Vasco da Gama left Lisbon with 170 men in a fleet of four heavy ships, each carrying 20 guns and a variety of trade goods. As he rounded the Cape, da Gama found himself in completely uncharted waters. Even worse, Portuguese navigational aids based on astronomical calculations were useless in the unfamiliar skies of the Indian Ocean.

Landing in Malindi, da Gama hired the services of an Arab navigator-astronomer, reputed to be one of the finest pilots of his time:

> Vasco da Gama, after he had a discussion with him, was greatly satisfied with his knowledge: principally, when he [the pilot] showed him a chart of the whole of the coast of India drawn, in the fashion of the Moors, that is with meridians and parallels . . . And when da Gama showed him a large astrolabe of wood which he had with him, and others of metal with which he measured the altitude of the sun, the pilot expressed no surprise, saying that some navigators of the Red Sea used brass instruments of triangular shape and quadrants with which they measured the altitude of the sun and principally of the Pole Star which they most commonly used in navigation.

These techniques were completely unknown to European navigators. Jewish astronomical expertise had taken the Portuguese as far as the Cape. Now Islamic navigational skill would finally help them reach India.

Not only did the Arabic pilot provide da Gama with the navigational expertise required to sail across the Indian Ocean. He also unwittingly disclosed just how extensive the development of Arabic science and astronomy had become. Just as Ptolemy's classical texts on geography and astronomy had been transmitted from Alexandria to Constantinople, Italy, Germany, and Portugal, so they had also circulated eastwards via Damascus, Baghdad, and Samarkand. Mehmed the Conqueror's patronage of Ptolemy's *Geography* represented just one dimension of the vigorous tradition of Islamic astronomy and geography. In 1513 the Ottoman naval commander known as Piri Reis issued a world map that its author claimed 'is based mainly on twenty charts and mappa mundi, one of which is drawn in the time of Alexander the Great, and is known as *dja'grafiye*'. This was a reference to Ptolemy's *Geography*. Piri Reis also consulted 'new maps of the Chinese and the Indian Seas', plus 'one Arab map of India, four new Portuguese maps drawn according to the geometrical methods of India and China, and also the map of the western lands drawn by Columbus'. The Ottoman court in Istanbul was clearly keeping a close watch on developments in the western Atlantic.

Only the western portion of Piri Reis's map survives, but its detail suggests that the representation of the Indian Ocean would have been equally comprehensive in incorporating new Portuguese maps into the astronomical and navigational expertise of Islamic, Hindu, and Chinese pilots and scholars. Piri Reis's comments emphasize the extensive level of cultural exchange and circulation of knowledge that underpinned the Age of Discovery. Muslims, Hindus, and Christians were all trading information and ideas in an attempt to capture the political and commercial initiative.

Navigationally speaking, da Gama and his expedition believed that they were sailing into a new world. They soon discovered that culturally they were entering a surprisingly familiar world in which they were seen as dirty, violent, and technologically backward. Da Gama reached Calicut on the southern coast of India in May 1498, but the gifts that he had brought were more appropriate for trade in Guinea than ceremonial presentation to the elegant court of the Samorin of Calicut. When the local merchants saw da Gama's

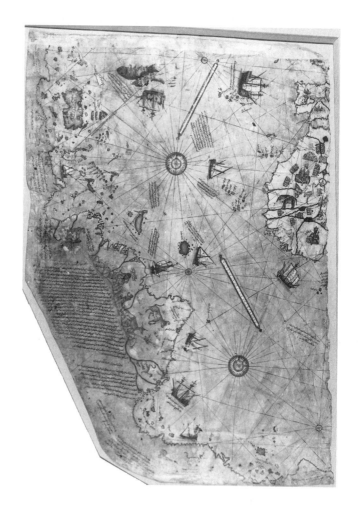

14. Piri Reis's world map (1513) shows how geographical information circulated between east and west

motley presentation of cloth, coral, sugar, oil, and honey, 'they laughed at it, saying it was not a thing to offer to a king, that the poorest merchant from Mecca, or from any other part of India gave more'. This inability to present suitable gifts produced political tensions and restricted the Portuguese to limited bartering. Nevertheless, the small but precious cargo of cinnamon, cloves, ginger, nutmeg, pepper, drugs, and precious stones and woods that da Gama presented upon his return to Lisbon in September 1499 convinced the Portuguese court that they had finally broken into the spice trade.

Portugal's entry into the trading emporium of the Indian Ocean was no more than a drop in the ocean. The region's ritualized patterns of trade and exchange and the sheer magnitude and diversity of its commodities dwarfed the supply and demand of the early Portuguese fleets. The Portuguese responded with a pragmatic accommodation and acceptance of different methods of exchange, exploitation of political differences between Hindu and Muslim communities, and the use of gunpowder in establishing limited commercial footholds throughout the region. However, back in Europe maps, books, and diplomatic exchanges reported da Gama's voyage as establishing Portugal's monopolization of the Asian spice trade.

The effect of the Portuguese commander's voyage was to transform the political map of the Renaissance world. Venice immediately attempted to sabotage discussions with Indian spice merchants who had arrived in Lisbon to discuss Portugal's role in the trade, and opened talks with both the Ottomans and the Egyptian Mamluks with the intention of using both diplomatic and military force to defend their commercial interests. In 1511 Portugal responded by negotiating with the Persian ruler Shah Ismail for a joint military attack on Egypt, that would strangle Venice's spice supply and help Ismail in his war with the Ottomans. As so often in the Renaissance, when trade and wealth were at stake, religious and ideological oppositions melted away.

Global ventures

By 1502, the first major phase of seaborne travel had reached its climax. Ptolemy's world picture had been shattered and a recognizably modern image of the world had started to emerge. The Portuguese had rounded Africa, reached India, accidentally discovered Brazil *en route* to the east (1500), and were pushing on to Malacca (1511), Hormuz (1513), China (1514), and Japan (1543). To the west Columbus's three voyages to the Americas had established a thriving trade in gold, silver, and slaves. In four voyages between 1497 and 1502, Amerigo Vespucci proved that Columbus had discovered a new continent. Disseminating his discoveries via the printing press, Vespucci ensured that it would be him and not Columbus who became synonymous in the European imagination with this new continent, America. Castile now had a separate continent to claim as its own, and an empire to build that could rival its Iberian neighbour.

With the revision of the European geographical imagination came a transformation in the texture of everyday life. The spices that flowed back into Europe affected what and how people ate, as did the influx of coconuts, oranges, yams, and bananas (from the east) and pineapples, groundnuts, papayas, and potatoes (from the Americas). The term 'spices' could also refer to a dizzying array of drugs (including opium, camphor, and cannabis), cosmetics, sugar, waxes, and cosmetics. Silk, cotton, and velvet changed what people wore, and musk and civet altered the way that they smelt. Dyes like indigo, vermilion, lac, saffron, and alum made Europe a brighter place, while porcelain, amber, ebony, sandalwood, ivory, bamboo, and lacquered wood all transformed the public and private domestic interiors of wealthy individuals. Tulips, parrots, rhinoceroses, chess sets, sexual appliances, and tobacco were just some of the more esoteric but prized goods that reached Europe from east and west. Lisbon itself was transformed into one of Europe's wealthiest cities, where it was possible to buy virtually anything. Princes displayed jewels, armour, statues, paintings, bezoar stones, and even parrots, monkeys, and horses in cabinets of curiosity, and Albrecht Dürer enthusiastically listed his acquisition of African salt cellars, Chinese porcelain, sandalwood, parrots, and Indian coconuts and feathers.

In 1513 the Portuguese finally reached the Moluccas, a small collection of islands in the Indonesian archipelago that provided the sole supply of cloves. This discovery provoked a serious political crisis. Since the Treaty of Tordesillas Portugal had pursued its commercial interests to the east, while Castile had concentrated on expansion to the west. This was fine when plotted on a flat map of the type obviously used under the terms of Tordesillas. But the discovery of the Moluccas posed the question of where such a line would fall in the eastern hemisphere if it were drawn all the way round the world on a globe.

Enter the Portuguese pilot, Fernão de Magalhães, better known today as Ferdinand Magellan. He suspected that a western passage to the Moluccas would be shorter than the Portuguese route via the Cape of Good Hope. However, in reviving Columbus's original idea of reaching the east by sailing west, Magellan faced the problem of Portuguese opposition to such a plan, so he offered the scheme to the Castilian king and future Habsburg Emperor Charles V. It was an ambitious commercial proposition that required investment in a long-distance voyage, a typical example of the motivation for so many Renaissance voyages of 'discovery'. Magellan's aim was not to circumnavigate the globe. His proposal was for a voyage that sailed westwards to the Moluccas, then came back via South America. This would claim the Moluccas for Castile on the basis of diplomatic and geographical precedent, cutting off Portugal's supply of top-quality spices and diverting Lisbon's wealth to Castile. Magellan's successful pitch for financial support was based on global thinking. He arrived in Seville in 1519 with 'a well-painted globe showing the entire world, and thereon traced the course he proposed to take'. Globes, not maps, were now the objects that most accurately captured the political and commercial geography of the 16th-century world.

Magellan quickly convinced Castile. He set sail in September 1519. Sailing down the coast of South America, Magellan had to suppress mutiny, and lost two ships searching for a way through the strait at the tip of South America that now bears his name. He spent weeks sailing across a Pacific Ocean that was larger than his maps suggested. The fleet finally reached Samar in the Philippines in April 1521, where Magellan got embroiled in a petty local conflict, and was killed alongside forty of his men. The remnants of the fleet set sail again and finally reached the Moluccas where they loaded cloves, pepper, ginger, nutmeg, and sandalwood. Unable to face the planned return journey through Magellan's Strait, the crew agreed to return via the Cape of Good Hope, running the risk of capture by patrolling Portuguese ships. Their decision made global history. On 8 September 1522 just 18 of the original crew of 240 arrived back in Seville, having completed the first recorded circumnavigation of the globe.

The news of Magellan's voyage caused diplomatic uproar. Charles V immediately interpreted the voyage as a justification for claiming that the Moluccas lay within his half of the globe. His advisers began to build a diplomatic and geographical case for possession. The Castilians cleverly used classical authority to support their claim. Ptolemy's overestimation of the size of Asia played into their hands. By repeating the inaccurate width of Asia in their maps, Castile pushed the Moluccas further east, and thus into their half of the globe. The Castilians submitted maps and globes where 'the description and figure of Ptolemy and the description and model found recently by those who came from the spice regions are alike . . . therefore Sumatra, Malacca and the Moluccas fall within our demarcation'.

As the two crowns sat down for their final attempt to resolve the dispute at Saragossa in 1529, Castile employed the Portuguese cartographer Diogo Ribeiro to make a series of maps and globes that placed the Moluccas within the Castilian half of the globe. This was the moment at which the Renaissance world went global in a recognizably modern sense. The consequences of Magellan's voyage meant that terrestrial globes became far more convincing representations of the shape and scope of the world.

While such globes did not survive, Ribeiro's world map dated 1529 remains as testimony to the manipulation of geographical reality that characterized the dispute. Ribeiro placed the Moluccas 172 and a half degrees west of the Tordesillas line – just seven and a half degrees inside the Castilian sphere. The map gave Charles V the negotiating power he needed. He sold his rights to the island back to the hapless Portuguese. Charles had in fact realized that short-term cash was preferable to a long-term commercial investment, because of the formidable cost and logistics of establishing a western trade route to the Moluccas. Ribeiro established himself as Castile's most respected cartographer, guessing that his geographical sleight of hand would never be discovered, because without an accurate method for calculating longitude, it would be impossible to ever fix the exact position of the Moluccas.

New worlds, old stories

With Columbus's discovery of America, the gold and silver that had started to flow back into the coffers of Charles's Habsburg Empire began to dwarf the revenue of the eastern spice trade. Where Portugal had established trading posts throughout the east, which demanded new mechanisms of trade and exchange, Spain used its military power to turn America into one large slave and mining colony.

In 1521 Hernando Cortes reached Tenochtitlán (modern-day Mexico City), the capital of the Aztec Empire; this he systematically destroyed, killing most of its inhabitants in the process, including its emperor, Montezuma. In 1533 the adventurer Francisco Pizarro

15. Diogo Ribeiro's 1529 Planisphere manipulated geographical knowledge to place the Moluccas Islands in the Habsburg half of the globe

led a handful of *conquistadores* and horses in the occupation of
Cuzco (now in modern Peru), the capital of the Incan Empire. The
indigenous population had little commercial or military power to
oppose the violent depredations of the Spaniards, who imposed a
quasi-feudal arrangement upon conquered regions, known as
encomienda. This involved the division of small local communities
amongst Spanish overseers, who provided a brutally exploitative
'livelihood' (in effect exacting unpaid hard labour) and Christian
education.

Conservative estimates calculate that, of a world population of
approximately 400 million in 1500, roughly 80 million inhabited
the Americas. By 1550, the population of the Americas was just 10
million. At the start of the 16th century Mexico's population has
been estimated at 25 million. In 1600, it had been reduced to one
million. European diseases such as smallpox and measles wiped out
most of the indigenous population, but warfare, slaughter, and
terrible treatment accounted for many fatalities. The romance of
discovering piles of gold and silver had quickly turned into a dirty,
murderous business of mining and enslavement.

The Spanish exploitation of the Americas had a direct impact on the
economy of Europe. Initially, gold flowed back into Europe from
Hispaniola and Central America. However, the conquests of Mexico
and Peru soon tipped the balance in favour of silver mining.
Between 1543 and 1548 silver deposits were found at Zacatecas and
Guanajuato north of Mexico City; in 1543 the Spaniards discovered
the infamous sugarloaf mountain of silver at Potosí in Bolivia. The
decisive breakthrough came in 1555 with the discovery of the
mercury amalgamation process, which allowed the creation of
much purer silver through the smelting of silver ore with mercury.
The result was a massive influx of silver into Europe. By the end of
the 16th century over 270,000 kg of silver and approximately 2,000
kg of gold were reaching Europe every year, compounding the rise
in inflation, and thereby contributing to what economic historians
have called a 'price revolution', as wages and the cost of living

soared, providing the framework for the long-term development of European capitalism.

The American mines and estates required workers, and the decimation of the local population soon meant that the Spanish needed another source of labour. Their solution was slaves. In 1510 King Ferdinand of Castile authorized the export of 50 African slaves, to the mines of Hispaniola. Alonso Zuazo wrote from there to Charles V in 1518, concerned at the work rate of the Indians. He recommended the 'import of *negros*, ideal people for the work here, in contrast to the natives, who are so feeble that there are only suitable for light work'. Between 1529 and 1537 the Castilian crown issued 360 licences to carry slaves from Africa to the New World. Thus began one of the most ignominious features of the Renaissance, as African slaves, kidnapped or bought for 50 pesos each by Portuguese 'merchants' in West Africa, were crammed into boats and shipped to the New World. There they were sold for double their purchase price and set to work in mines and on estates. Between 1525 and 1550 approximately 40,000 slaves were shipped from Africa to the Americas, enriching Europe but devastating African communities.

Not all Spaniards endorsed the slaughter and oppression that took place in the Americas. The Franciscan Fray Motolinia believed that 'if anyone should ask what has been the cause of so many evils, I would answer: covetousness'. Bartolomé de Las Casas similarly argued, 'I do not say that they want to kill them [Indians] directly, from the hate they bear them; they kill them because they want to be rich and have much gold'. Philosophically, the discovery of a New World also transformed European understanding of its own cultural superiority. In 'On the Cannibals', published in his *Essays* of 1580, the humanist Michel de Montaigne claimed to have spoken at length with several Brazilian Indians. He concluded 'there is nothing savage or barbarous about those peoples, but that every man calls barbarous anything that he is not accustomed to'. Montaigne developed a highly sceptical and relativistic approach to perceptions of 'civilization' and 'barbarism', arguing that 'we can indeed call those folk barbarians by the rules of reason but not in comparison with ourselves, who surpass them in every kind of barbarism'.

The discovery of America revolutionized Renaissance Europe's world picture. It had confounded deeply entrenched classical philosophical and religious beliefs that simply could not accommodate the existence of the culture, language, and belief systems of the indigenous inhabitants. It was partly responsible for defining Europe's shift from a medieval world to a more recognizably modern world. However, the discovery of America brought together a volatile fear of the new and the unknown with a desire for unlimited wealth that ignored the incredible suffering and oppression inflicted upon indigenous people and slaves in the Americas. Its legacy can be seen in the poverty and political instability of much of South America today, and the inequalities of wealth and opportunity that characterize so much of the modern global economy.

Chapter 5
Science and philosophy

Come, Mephistopheles, let us dispute again,

And reason of divine astrology.

Speak, are there many spheres above the moon?

Are all celestial bodies but one globe,

As is the substance of this centric earth?

(Faustus, in Christopher Marlowe, *Doctor Faustus*, c.1592)

Christopher Marlowe's *Doctor Faustus* dramatizes the excitement and danger associated with the rise of science and speculative thought in the Renaissance. Faustus is a learned 'astrologer' who has reached the limits of the study of astronomy, anatomy, and philosophy. In seeking magical powers of life over death, Faustus sells his soul to the devil Mephistopheles. Given a chance to repent, he refuses. He is more interested in questioning Mephistopheles on the controversial topic of 'divine astrology'. Faustus is ultimately damned and falls to hell. But his preference for learning and contempt for religion caught the late Renaissance popular imagination. His fate encapsulates modern anxieties about the ethics of scientific experimentation. This ambivalence (we want to know, but can we know too much?) captures the mood of the transformations in popular and applied science that took place in the 15th and 16th centuries. The individual's relationship to his/her mind, body, and environment were all transformed as a result of renewed scientific collaboration in the pursuit of practical problem-solving, exchanges of ideas between cultures, and the impact of new technologies.

From macrocosm to microcosm

Once Faustus has sold his soul, he asks Mephistopheles for a book 'where I might see all characters and planets of the heavens'. The most controversial book that Faustus could have consulted was *On the Revolutions of the Celestial Spheres* by the Polish canon and astronomer Nicolaus Copernicus. First printed in Nuremberg in May 1543, Copernicus's revolutionary book overturned the medieval belief that the earth lay at the centre of the universe. Copernicus's vision of the heavens showed that the earth, along with all the other known planets, rotated around the sun. Copernicus subtly revised the work of classical Greek and Arabic astronomy scholars. He argued that 'they did not achieve their aim, which we hope to reach by accepting the fact that the earth moves'.

Copernicus tried to limit the revolutionary significance of his ideas by accommodating them within a classical scientific tradition. But the Catholic Church was horrified and condemned the book. Copernicus's argument overturned the biblical belief that the earth – and humanity with it – stood at the centre of the universe. It was a liberating but dangerous idea.

Within a month of the publication of Copernicus's treatise, another book was printed that would transform another area of science: Andreas Vesalius's *On the Structure of the Human Body*. Published in Basle in June 1543, Vesalius's book marked the beginning of modern observational science and anatomy. Its title-page depicts Vesalius conducting a graphic public anatomy lesson, held in a 'theatre', surrounded by students, citizens, and fellow physicians. Vesalius returns our gaze as he peels back the female cadaver's abdomen. This gesture invites the reader to open the book and follow the anatomist as he reduces the human body to the skeleton that hovers above the dissected body. Vesalius revealed the mystery of the inner body as a complex map of flesh, blood, and bone, a potentially infinite source of study. His exploration of the secrets of the human body opened the way for the later 16th-century study of

net, in quo terram cum orbe lunari tanquam epicyclo contineri diximus. Quinto loco Venus nono mense reducitur. Sextum denicq; locum Mercurius tenet, octuaginta dierum spacio circu currens. In medio uero omnium residet Sol. Quis enim in hoc

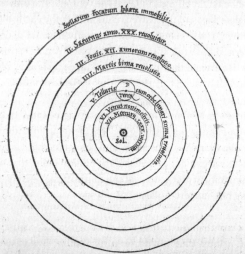

pulcherimo templo lampadem hanc in alio uel meliori loco po neret, quàm unde totum simul possit illuminare? Siquidem non inepte quidam lucernam mundi, alij mentem, alij rectorem uo cant. Trimegistus uisibilem Deum, Sophoclis Electra intuenté omnia. Ita profecto tanquam in solio regali Sol residens circum agentem gubernat Astrorum familiam. Tellus quoq; minime fraudatur lunari ministerio, sed ut Aristoteles de animalibus ait, maximâ Luna cũ terra cognationé habet. Concipit interea à Sole terra, & impregnatur annuo partu. Inuenimus igitur sub hac

16. Nicolaus Copernicus's heliocentric system from his *On the Revolutions of the Celestial Spheres* (1543). For the first time the sun ('Sol') lies at the centre of the cosmos

the ear, the female reproductive organs, the venous system, and, in 1628, William Harvey's theory of the circulation of the blood.

Vesalius's anatomical studies were based on methodical observation and analysis of empirical reality. For Vesalius this meant stealing the bodies of the condemned and the diseased, as he confessed: 'I was not afraid to snatch in the middle of the night what I so longed for.' While Vesalius discovered the microscopic secrets of the human body, Copernicus explored the macrocosmic mysteries of the universe. The implications were profound. Copernicus ultimately transformed scientific apprehensions of time and space by undermining the notion of a divinely ordered world. Instead, the earth was envisaged as one planet amongst the vast time and space of the universe. Vesalius envisaged the individual as an infinitely complex and intricate mechanism of blood, flesh, and bone that Shakespeare's Hamlet would later regard as a 'quintessence of dust' and the philosopher René Descartes would call a 'moving machine'.

Alongside Copernicus and Vesalius came hundreds of publications that began to define the emerging disciplines of scientific enquiry: mathematics, physics, biology, the natural sciences, and geography. Luca Pacioli's *Everything about Arithmetic, Geometry and Proportion* (1494) was the first account of the practical application of arithmetic and geometry, one of 214 mathematical books published in Italy between 1472 and 1500. In 1545 the astrologer Geronimo Cardano published his *Great Art*, the first contemporary European book of algebra. In 1537 Niccolò Tartaglia issued his *New Science*, dealing with physics, followed by his study of arithmetic, *A General Treatise on Numbers and Measurement* (1556). In the natural sciences Leonhard Fuchs's *History of Plants* (1542) studied over 500 plants, whilst Conrad Gesner's *History of Animals* (1551–8) contained hundreds of illustrations that redefined zoology. In geography, experiments in new ways of mapping the world culminated in Gerard Mercator's 1569 world map: his famous projection is still used today.

17. The title-page to Andreas Vesalius's *On the Structure of the Human Body* (1543), where the drama of anatomical dissection is carried out as if in a theatre

Renaissance scientific innovation was invariably tied to practical requirements, and nowhere more than in the field of warfare. Niccolò Tartaglia's publications on mechanics, dynamics, and motion represented the first modern studies of ballistics. His *Various Queries and Inventions* (1546) was dedicated to the militarily ambitious Henry VIII, and dealt with ballistics as well as the creation and use of artillery. Tartaglia's work responded to and further developed new inventions in weaponry and warfare, from the innovation of using gunpowder as a propellant in the early 14th century to the emergence of cavalry as a decisive factor in 16th-century conflict. The impact of such military-scientific developments led to further advancements in the fields of anatomy and surgery. In 1545 Ambroise Paré, a great admirer of Vesalius, published his study of surgery based on his involvement in the Franco-Habsburg wars of the 1540s. Paré disproved the popular belief that gunshot wounds were poisonous and rejected the dressing of wounds in boiling oil, a practical innovation that subsequently earned him the epithet of the father of modern surgery.

Geometry and mathematics also provided new ways of understanding the increasingly elaborate and often invisible movement of commodities and paper money across the globe, but they also enabled new developments in ship design, surveying, and map-making, which anticipated ever more rapid commercial transactions of a speed and volume hitherto unimaginable. Regiomontanus's book *On Triangles* became crucial to 16th-century map-makers and navigators. Its sophisticated treatment of spherical trigonometry allowed cartographers to construct terrestrial globes and map projections that took into account the curvature of the earth's surface. The first printed edition was published in 1533 in Nuremberg, the home of the early terrestrial globe industry that emerged in the aftermath of the first circumnavigation of the globe in 1522.

Scientific innovation in mathematics, astronomy, and geometry enabled increasingly ambitious long-distance travel and commerce both eastwards and westwards, which in itself created new opportunities as well as new problems. Encountering new people, plants, animals, and minerals throughout Africa, south-east Asia, and the Americas enlarged and redefined the domains of European physiology, botany, zoology, and mineralogy. These developments often had a specifically commercial dimension. Georgius Agricola's *De Re Metallica*, first published in 1556, dealt with 'Digging of ore', 'Smelting', 'Separation of silver from gold, and of lead from gold and silver', and the 'Manufacture of salt, soda, alum, vitriol, sulphur, bitumen, and glass'. The combination of chemistry, mineralogy, and Agricola's observations and experiences of the mining communities of southern Germany revolutionized mining techniques, and played a crucial role in the massive increase in the production and export of New World silver in the latter half of the 16th century.

Merchants and financiers soon realized that investing in science could be a profitable business. In 1519 the German humanist Ulrich von Hutton wrote a treatise on guaiacum, a new wonder drug from the Americas that was believed to cure syphilis. Dedicating his book to the archbishop of Mainz, Hutton wrote, 'I hope that Your Eminence has escaped the pox but should you catch it (Heaven forbid but you can never tell) I would be glad to treat and heal you'. It was believed (mistakenly) that syphilis originated in the New World and returned to Europe with Columbus in 1493, and that the geographical origin of the disease had to provide the cure. The German merchant house of Fugger, which held an import monopoly on the drug, began a campaign to endorse guaiacum, opening a chain of hospitals exclusively supplying the drug. As the price climbed and its uselessness became apparent, the Swiss physician and alchemist Paracelsus published a series of attacks on guaiacum, denouncing it as a commercial scam, and recommending the more painful use of mercury.

Paracelsus rejected the classical belief in humoral theory, which believed in maintaining a balance between the body's four constituent fluids: blood, yellow bile, phlegm, and black bile. Instead, he took a more alchemical approach to medicine, arguing that the basic components of Nature could be matched to specific diseases, which led him to use elements like iron, sulphur, and mercury in his treatment of diseases like syphilis. In drawing on the new practical world of trial and error, as well as chemistry, Paracelsus clashed with institutional and financial authorities. The Fuggers responded to his work on syphilis and mercury by using their financial muscle to suppress his publications and ridicule his scientific credibility. These conflicts anticipated the rise of the modern pharmaceutical industry, and the world of patent medicine.

Science from the east

Renaissance science also received added impetus from the increased transmission of knowledge between east and west. Many of the classical Greek scientific texts survived in Arabic, Persian, and Hebrew translations and were revised in places like Toledo in Spain and the Academy of Science established in Baghdad in the 9th century. Islamic centres of learning were crucial in driving forward scientific advances based on both Greek learning and Arabic innovations, particularly in the fields of medicine and astronomy. As early as the 1140s Hugo of Santalla, a Latin translator of Arabic texts, wrote, 'it befits us to imitate the Arabs especially, for they are as it were our teachers and the pioneers'.

Arabic studies of medicine directly affected the dissemination of knowledge in the west. The 10th-century Arabic scholar Avicenna studied the Greek medical treatises of Galen and Aristotle in composing his encyclopedic book the *Canon of Medicine*. He defined medicine as 'the science by which we learn the various states of the human body, when in health and when not in health, whereby health is conserved and whereby it is restored after being lost'. The *Canon* was translated into Latin in Toledo in the 12th century by Gerard of Cremona. The translation generated over 30 printed editions in Italy between 1500 and 1550, as Avicenna's book became a set medical text in universities throughout Europe.

In 1527 the Venetian physician Andrea Alpago published a new edition of the *Canon* based on his experience as physician to the Venetian consulate in Damascus. Alpago also studied the writings of the Syrian physician Ibn al-Nafis (1213–88), whose research on the pulmonary movement of the blood influenced 16th-century European investigations of circulation. Vesalius condemned academic physicians who spent their time 'unworthily decrying Avicenna and the rest of the Arabic writers'. He was so convinced of the importance of Arabic medicine that he began to learn the language himself, and wrote commentaries praising the therapeutics and materia medica of al-Razi ('Rhazes'). In 1531 Otto Brunfels, the so-called 'father of botany', edited a printed edition of the 9th-century materia medica of Ibn Sarabiyun (Serapion the younger), which had a decisive influence on his own understanding of botany.

In astronomy and geography, Arabic scholars were particularly instrumental in translating the crucial works of the Greek cosmographer Ptolemy. His *Almagest* and *Geography* were translated from Greek into Arabic, criticized, and then revised in Toledo, Baghdad, and Samarkand. After the fall of Constantinople in 1453, the Ottoman Sultan Mehmed the Conqueror proved to be an enthusiastic patron of Ptolemy. He commissioned the Greek scholar Georgius Amirutzes to revise Ptolemy's text in Arabic. The world map, completed in 1465, is an amalgamation of Ptolemy's calculations with more up-to-date Arabic, Greek, and Latin geographical information. With south oriented at its top, scales of latitude, and a complex conical projection, this was a cutting-edge world map.

Scientific transactions between east and west also contributed to Copernicus's account of the heliocentric nature of the solar system. One of the most important centres of Arabic astronomy and mathematics was established at the Maragha observatory in Persia in the mid-13th century. Its leading figure was Nasīr ad-Dīn al-Ṭūsī

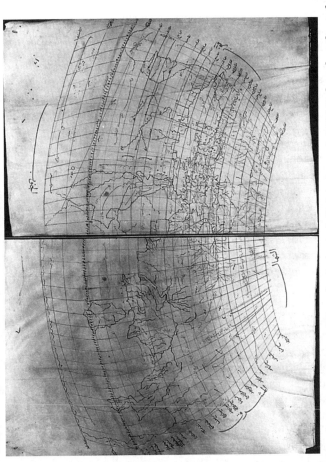

18. Mehmed the Conqueror commissioned Georgius Amirutzes's Ptolemaic map in 1465. It shows how the study of Ptolemy developed in the east as well as the west

(1201–74) whose *Memoir on Astronomy* (*Tadhkira fī 'ilm al'haya*) modified Ptolemy's contradictory work on the motion of the spheres. Tusi's most important revision of Ptolemy led to the creation of the 'Tusi couple'. This theorem states that linear motion can be derived from uniform circular motion, which Tusi demonstrated using one sphere rolling inside another of twice the radius. Historians of astronomy have now realized that Copernicus reproduced the Tusi couple in his *Revolutions*, and that the theorem was crucial in defining his heliocentric vision of the solar system. Nobody looked for Arabic influence upon Renaissance science because the assumption was that there was nothing to find.

The art of science

The printing press brought together art and science as never before, and one of the individuals who capitalized on this situation was Albrecht Dürer. He quickly mastered the new technique of copperplate engraving, and travelled to Italy 'to learn the secrets of the art of perspective'. He believed that 'the new art must be based upon science – in particular, upon mathematics, as the most exact, logical, and graphically constructive of the sciences'. In 1525 he published a treatise on geometry and perspective entitled *A Course in the Art of Measurement with Compass and Ruler*, to 'benefit not only the painters but also goldsmiths, sculptors, stonemasons, carpenters and all those who have to rely on measurement'.

Dürer's book explained the application of the new science of perspective and optics. It also contained illustrations of 'drawing machines' that could be used to impose the grid of perspective upon the subject. One of his illustrations shows the draughtsman using a sight to locate his subject on a piece of paper. The grid-like structure of the artist's plate corresponds to the glass panel that separates draughtsman from model. The draughtsman simply copies every point on the glass onto the corresponding grid reference on his plate. Dürer's illustration shares many similarities with the female cadaver whose womb is ripped open for the edification of a roomful

19. Dürer's draughtsman gazing at a naked woman through a 'drawing machine', from his *Course in the Art of Measurement*, printed in 1525

of men in Vesalius's *Studies*. For both Dürer and Vesalius, women have no part to play in this artistic and scientific revolution, other than as objects for dissection or mute, sexually available models.

An early influence on Dürer's career was the figure who has come to personify the relations between art and science in the Renaissance: Leonardo da Vinci. Luca Pacioli claimed that Leonardo was the 'most worthy of painters, perspectivists, architects and musicians, one endowed with every perfection', who utilized his immersion in science to market his skills as a sculptor, surveyor, military engineer, and anatomical draughtsman. Leonardo's ability to combine artistic skills with practical scientific ability made his services highly prized by several powerful patrons.

In 1482 Duke Ludovico Sforza of Milan employed Leonardo as a military engineer on the basis of a curriculum vitae that emphasized his practical abilities:

> I have plans for very light, strong, and easily portable bridges ... I have methods for destroying every fortress ... I will make canon, mortar, and light ordnance ... I will assemble catapults, mangonels, trebuckets, and other instruments ... I believe I can give complete satisfaction in the field of architecture, and the construction of both public and private buildings ... Also I can execute sculpture in marble, bronze, and clay.

Ludovico discarded Leonardo's fanciful military science, commissioning him instead to cast an immense equestrian monument that, as Leonardo claimed, 'will be to the immortal glory and eternal honour . . . of the illustrious house of Sforza'. Leonardo's sketches of the proportions and casting of the horse show that he used all his skill in hydraulics, anatomy, and design to design a statue for the civic glorification of the Sforza.

Like most of his technically ambitious projects, Leonardo's horse was never built. He moved on and by 1504 he was in negotiations with the Ottoman Sultan Bayezid II to build a 350-metre bridge over the Bosphorus. 'I will erect it high as an arch', Leonardo wrote to Bayezid, 'so that a ship under full sail could sail underneath it'. Exasperated at Leonardo's unrealistic designs, Bayezid dropped him and opened negotiations with Michelangelo. One of Leonardo's great miscalculations was not committing his ideas to print. As a result, unlike Dürer, Leonardo left no concrete innovations to posterity. He remained a brilliant but enigmatic figure until being rescued from obscurity by Walter Pater in the 19th century.

Natural philosophy

There was no divide between science, philosophy, and magic in the 15th century. All three came under the general heading of 'natural philosophy'. Central to the development of natural philosophy was the recovery of classical authors, most importantly the work of Aristotle and Plato. At the beginning of the 15th century Aristotle remained the basis for all scholastic speculation on philosophy and science. Kept alive in the Arabic translations and commentaries of Averroës and Avicenna, Aristotle provided a systematic perspective on mankind's relationship with the natural world. Surviving texts like his *Physics*, *Metaphysics*, and *Meteorology* provided scholars with the logical tools to understand the forces that created the natural world. Mankind existed within this world as a mortal 'political animal' destined to forge social communities thanks to his ability to reason above and beyond any other animal. From the early

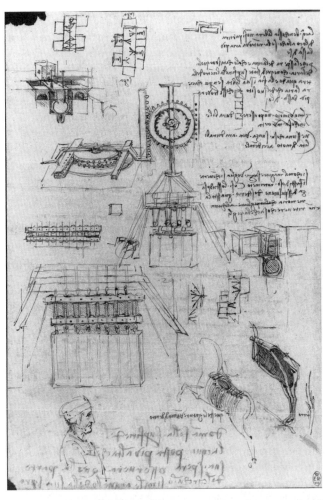

20. Leonardo's studies for a casting pit for the Sforza horse completed in 1498. The statue was never finished

15th century, humanist scholars began to translate Aristotle into Latin and discover new texts such as the *Poetics* and the pseudo-Aristotelian *Mechanics*. Engineers in building and construction utilized the *Mechanics* with its description of motion and mechanical devices. In the world of political and domestic management Leonardo Bruni translated the *Politics*, *Nicomachean Ethics*, and *Oeconomicus*, the latter a study of estates and household organization, which he argued were central to the civic organization of 15th-century Italian society.

As humanist scholars began to publish new translations and commentaries on Aristotle, they also recovered a whole range of neglected classical authors and philosophical perspectives, most significantly exponents of Stoicism, Scepticism, Epicureanism, and Platonism. The most decisive development was the recovery and translation of the works of Aristotle's teacher, Plato. The mystical, idealist Platonism of Marsilio Ficino, Nicholas of Cusa, and Giovanni Pico della Mirandola argued that, contrary to Aristotle's belief, the soul was immortal, and aspired to a cosmic unity and love of ultimate truth. Imprisoned in its earthly body, the soul, according to Ficino in his *Platonic Theology* (1474), 'tries to liken itself to God'. Ficino argued that Plato

> deemed it just and pious that the human mind, which receives everything from God, should give everything back to him. Thus, if we devote ourselves to moral philosophy, he exhorts us to purify our soul so that it may eventually become unclouded, permitting it to see the divine light and worship of God.

This Platonic approach had two distinct advantages over Aristotelianism. First, it could be accommodated much more easily into 15th-century Christian belief in the immortality of the soul and the individual's worship of God. Secondly, it defined philosophical speculation as an individual's most precious possession. Ficino's version of Platonism cleverly elevated his own profession as philosopher. Its rejection of politics in favour of mystical contemplation also suited the political philosophy of Ficino's patron, the Florentine ruler Cosimo de' Medici, who appointed Ficino as head of his philosophical academy in 1463.

Subsequent philosophers rapidly expanded and refined Ficino's Neoplatonism. In the introduction to his *Conclusiones* (1486), Giovanni Pico della Mirandola attempted to create what he called 'the concord of Plato and Aristotle', in an attempt to unify classical philosophy with Christianity. Pico drew on mystical Jewish and Arabic texts (he started learning Arabic in acknowledgement of the significance of Arab philosophy) to establish natural philosophy as the best method of metaphysical enquiry. 'Natural philosophy' he claimed, 'will allay the strife and differences of opinion which vex, distract, and wound the spirit'. Unfortunately, Pico's *Conclusiones* were investigated by a papal commission that condemned some of his theses as heretical. Later scholars of the Renaissance were more interested in Pico's introductory remarks to the *Conclusiones*, which they identified as providing a new vision of individual selfhood. Drawing on Plato, Pico argued in his introduction that man is 'the maker and moulder of thyself', with the liberty 'to have what he wishes, to be whatever he wills'. For 19th-century writers like Walter Pater, Pico's introduction became the classic statement on individuality and the birth of Renaissance man, and in 1882 it was given its English title, *Oration on the Dignity of Man*, a phrase that Pico himself never used.

Both Plato and Aristotle continued to exert an enormous influence upon the art, literature, philosophy, and science of the 16th century. Neoplatonism inspired the artistic and literary work of figures as diverse as Michelangelo, Erasmus, and Spenser, while Aristotelianism remained a sufficiently diverse body of work to allow scientists and philosophers to revise it in line with their expanding world. However, as the century drew to a close, the intellectual primacy of both philosophers was slowly but surely eroded. The discovery of America led Montaigne to realize in 1580 that the work of Aristotle and Plato 'cannot apply to these new lands'. Galileo's refutation of Aristotle's theories of motion, acceleration, and the nature of the universe in the early 17th century led him to conclude 'I greatly doubt that Aristotle ever tested by experiment'.

Sir Francis Bacon, who also shared Galileo's rejection of Aristotle, began to argue for empirical observation in scientific analysis. By 1620 Bacon was calling for a 'Great Instauration' of learning, where 'philosophy and the sciences may no longer float in air, but rest on the solid foundation of experience of every kind, and the same well examined and weighed'. Bacon's *Novum Organum*, or *The New Organon*, offered a direct rebuttal of Aristotle's *Organon*, or *Instrument for Rational Thinking*, from where Bacon took his title. Aristotle had argued for the use of syllogisms in logical reasoning, where two incontrovertible premises (for instance, all humans are mortal, and all Greeks are human) logically infer a particular conclusion (all Greeks are mortal). In this scheme, theory and rhetoric are regarded as more reliable than practice or experience. Bacon turned this scheme on its head. He argued that Aristotle's basic, accepted premises required interrogation, and what he called

> a new logic, teaching to invent and judge by induction (as finding syllogism incompetent for sciences of nature) and thereby to make philosophy and the sciences both more true and more active.

Bacon proposed a completely new vision of scientific knowledge based on the careful compilation of natural data based on observation, experimentation, and induction; in other words, deriving general theoretical principles from particular facts. It was a massive undertaking of the reformation of the classification of the natural sciences that remained incomplete at the time of his death, but it broke with the classical assumptions revered by Renaissance scholars, and anticipated the experimental science carried out by the Royal Society in the later decades of the 17th century. In 1626 Bacon completed his *New Atlantis*, a utopian world that drew on

Plato, but whose most valued citizens were no longer philosophers but experimental scientists. It was a shift that would influence modern science and its break with philosophy.

Chapter 6
Rewriting the Renaissance

'Renaissance literature': the term is as misleading and anachronistic as phrases we have already encountered like 'Renaissance humanism' and 'Renaissance science'. Petrarch, Machiavelli, More, and Bacon were politicians and diplomats whose writings have only subsequently been labelled 'Renaissance literature', and who are now studied in university literature departments across the world. It is only towards the end of the 16th century that the concept of the professional writer develops with the growth of the theatre in countries like Spain and England, and the financial success of printing, that allowed poets and pamphleteers to consider creative writing as a full-time career. The different types of literary expression – poetry, drama, and prose – responded to these social and political changes in a variety of ways, all of which had regionally specific manifestations. What we now call Renaissance literature was written predominantly in the various European vernacular languages: English, French, Italian, Spanish, and German. The story of such literary developments involves writers detaching themselves from the international, classical languages of the elite (Greek, Arabic, and in particular Latin) and choosing to write in their particular vernacular languages. Because of the difficulty of doing justice to these specific vernacular traditions, in what follows my emphasis falls on the development of poetry, prose, and drama in specific relation to the English language.

Poetry

Alongside epic, lyric poetry was esteemed as the pinnacle of literary creativity in the Renaissance. The rise of courtly culture in Italy and northern Europe provided scope for the cultivated sensibility of lyric poetry, with its focus on a beloved mistress, whilst also reflecting on the subjective status of the lover-poet. One of its most influential pioneers was the humanist scholar Petrarch. His writing of *Il Canzoniere*, a collection of 365 poems written between 1327 and 1374, drew on Dante's collection of lyrics the *New Life*. Petrarch refined the sonnet, a heavily stylized poem of 14 lines, broken down into two sections (the octave, or first eight lines, and sestet, or final six lines) with a highly specific rhyme structure. The Petrarchan sonnet idealized the female subject at the same time as it explored the emotional complexity of the poet's identity. Petrarch complained in one sonnet that 'In this state, Lady I am because of you'. This intimate, introspective poetic style, which allowed the poet to explore his own moral state in relation to either his beloved or his religion (and the two were often conflated) came to influence courtly Renaissance culture and poetry throughout the 15th and 16th centuries.

The tradition developed in Italy in the poetry of Cardinal Bembo, in Spain with Garcilaso de la Vega, in France with Joachim du Bellay and Pierre de Ronsard, and in England with Sir Thomas Wyatt's mid-16th century translations of Petrarch into vernacular English. This English tradition culminated in Shakespeare's sonnet sequence (*c*.1600) that parodied the Petrarchan convention with its famous line, 'my mistress' eyes are nothing like the sun' (Sonnet 130). In his sonnets Shakespeare went beyond Petrarch by adding a third dimension to the relationship between the poet and his mistress: a male rival. This triangulated relationship, expressed in supple, punning vernacular English, was unprecedented. It allowed Shakespeare to address male rivalry and the problems of literary patronage and domestic service, 'Desiring this man's art and that man's scope' (Sonnet 29) and to explore the corrosive effects of sexual desire, 'Th' expense of spirit in a waste of shame' (Sonnet 129).

In Sonnet 134 the poet admits to having lost his mistress to his male friend:

> So, now I have confessed that he is thine,
> And I myself am mortgaged to thy will,
> Myself I'll forfeit, so that other mine
> Thou wilt restore to be my comfort still.

The poet hopes to retain at least his male friendship with his rival, but the poem concludes that even this is impossible: 'Him have I lost; thou hast both him and me; / He pays the whole, and yet am I not free'. The poet is 'mortgaged' to his mistress, and offers to 'forfeit' himself to preserve his friend, but in the end even the friend is in the sexual grip of the mistress. The poet hopes his friend will settle the debt, or pay 'the whole', but the pun here is on whole/hole – a graphic sexual image that reveals the power of the woman to 'ensnare' both men. The sonnet's language draws on the specifically Elizabethan experience of legal obligation and financial indebtedness. Its execution is peculiarly English in its rhyme and punning. Shakespeare has moved a long way from the Latinate and classical influence of Petrarch. His poetry anticipates the development of later English poets like the Metaphysical Poets, and signals a departure from the Renaissance style of poetic utterance to the national vernacular traditions of the later 17th century.

Kidnapping language: women respond

While the poetry of Petrarch celebrated women as idealized but silent paragons of chaste virtue, Shakespeare's sonnets reflected an increasing anxiety about women's contradictory status in a male-dominated culture. Some women responded by taking advantage of the changing nature of humanist education and the rise of printing to offer a different version of femininity. Their writing suggests that many of the assumptions about relations between the sexes were more actively contested than the predominantly male literary canon has led us to believe.

Throughout the 16th century a range of women writers appropriated Platonic and Petrarchan conventions to question male assumptions about women and to try to define their own personal and creative autonomy. In her *Rymes* (published posthumously in Lyons in 1545), Pernette du Guillet used Neoplatonic ideas and Petrarchan conventions to establish poetic equality with her male lover: 'just as I am yours / (And want to be), you are entirely mine' she claims in one poem. Elsewhere she attacks the fickleness and inequality of Petrarchan sentiment, assuring her female audience, 'Let's not be surprised / If our desires change'. This rejection of male poetic convention was taken even further by Louise Labé, whose poetic *Euvres* were also published in Lyons in 1555. Labé used the Petrarchan sonnet to criticize its objectification of women's bodies, turning the tables by asking 'What height makes a man worthy of admiration?' Rather than establishing her subservience to a fictionalized male lover, Labé competes with him, claiming in another reversal of Petrarchan convention 'I'd use the power of my eyes so well . . . That in no time I'd conquer him completely'.

This sexual frankness was combined with an insistence upon women's right to educational attainment and creative freedom. In *The Copy of a Letter* (1567) and *A Sweet Nosegay* (1573), the Elizabethan Isabella Whitney asserted some independence from the limitations of domestic life, arguing that 'til some household cares me tie, / My books and pen I will apply'. One poet who freed herself from the domestic limitations explored by Whitney was the Venetian courtesan Veronica Franco. *Rime*, her collection of poems published in 1575, both demystified the idealism of Petrarchan love from the perspective of a paid courtesan and argued that 'When we women, too, are armed and trained / We'll be able to stand up to any man'. Struggling with their relationship to the increasing religious persecution and political upheaval of mid-16th century Europe, writers like Franco and Whitney adapted male literary traditions to present a very different perspective on the nature of women.

Printed tales

Writers also took advantage of the relatively new medium of print to establish their distinctive literary voices. Print transformed literary expression, as it created demand amongst an increasingly literate and predominantly metropolitan audience that was looking for new forms to understand their changing world. In 1554 the Dominican friar Matteo Bandello published his *Novelle*, short stories of contemporary urban life that, according to their author, 'do not deal with connected history but are rather a miscellany of diverse happenings'. Giambattista Giraldi, more popularly known as Cinthio, printed another collection of equally influential novellas in 1565. The prologue to his *Hecatommithi* draws on the traumatic sack of Rome by Lutheran soldiers in 1527. The violent events are described in terms reminiscent of the tragic Roman dramatist Seneca, and Cinthio and Bandello's stories inspired some of the greatest and bloodiest tragedies performed on the Elizabethan and Jacobean stage, including Thomas Kyd's *Spanish Tragedy* (*c*.1587), Shakespeare's *Othello* (1603), and John Webster's *The White Devil* (*c*.1613). Like prose writing, the development of the theatre, particularly in England, was increasingly based on investment and profit rather than courtly patronage or religious piety, a situation that allowed for increasingly complex and naturalistic representations of society and the individual.

The flexibility of the printing process also allowed writers like François Rabelais to respond to criticism of his books and to insert contemporary events into later editions of his work. Rabelais published *Pantagruel* (1532) and *Gargantua* (1534), which recounted the comical adventures of two giants, Gargantua and his son Pantagruel. Rabelais uses the adventures of his giants to satirize and parody everything from the church to the new humanist learning. Writing in a fantastic 'copious' style that mixed learned languages with vernacular French, Rabelais's description of Pantagruel captures his abundant mixing of styles. Born to a mother 'who died in childbirth' because 'he was so amazingly large and so heavy that he could not come into the world without suffocating [her]', the young giant eats whole sheep and bears, causes a scholar to shit himself, and studies the new learning in a bewildering variety of newly printed books including *The Art of Farting* and *The Chimney-Sweep of Astrology*. Pantagruel also resolves a legal dispute between the Lords Kissmyarse and Suckfart and, in a parody of seaborne discovery and scientific innovation, he finally sails away to 'the port of Utopia'.

The four books of Gargantua and Pantagruel's adventures published in Rabelais's lifetime were enormously successful; in his prologue to *Pantagruel* Rabelais boasted 'more copies of it have been sold by the printers in two months than there will be of the Bible in nine years'. From 1533 the scholastics of the Sorbonne in Paris, who had been mercilessly satirized by Rabelais, took their revenge by condemning all his books as obscene and blasphemous. His publications were banned for the rest of his life. However, other writers adopted his irreverent, abundant style, including the English satirist and pamphleteer Thomas Nashe. In *The Unfortunate Traveller* (1594), Nashe recounts the picaresque wanderings of Jack Wilton, an itinerant page, across 16th-century Europe, embroiling himself in war, religious conflict, murder, rape, and imprisonment. Like Rabelais, Nashe uses the relatively new form of prose writing to turn the conventions of lyric and epic upside down. Instead of following the romance narrative of epic poets, Nashe's 'fantastical treatise' uses the scepticism and verbal dexterity of earlier humanists like More and Erasmus (who are introduced in the course of the narrative) to defy the moral strictures of more traditional literary conventions. In its exuberant mixing of styles and voices, Nashe's voice shares affinities with Miguel de Cervantes's *Don Quixote* (1604) and anticipates the subsequent development of the English novel. Daniel Defoe was one of many early English novelists who admired Nashe's work.

Epic

Epic poetry possessed a far more distinguished lineage than the relatively new and experimental prose fictions of Bandello, Cinthio, and Nashe. Homer's *Iliad* and *Odyssey*, and Virgil's *Aeneid* offered Renaissance poets classical models of empire-building and myths of national origin structured around the heroic wanderings of a central protagonist – in Homer, Odysseus, in Virgil, Aeneas. The rise of Italian city states in the 15th century, and the later development of the Portuguese, Habsburg, and English claims to global authority, gave epic poets the opportunity to rework the classical epic on a more contemporary global scale.

One of the most influential practitioners of the epic was Ludovico Ariosto, an ambassador to one of the greatest Italian dynasties of the 15th century, the Este of Ferrara. In the opening of his epic poem *Orlando Furioso* (1516) Ariosto announces, 'I sing of knights and ladies, of love and arms, of courtly chivalry, of courageous deeds – all from the time when the Moors crossed the sea from Africa and wrought havoc in France.' This was a backward-looking, chivalric poem about 8th-century conflict between the Christian knights of Emperor Charlemagne and the Saracens. Ariosto was unable to offer a more contemporary setting, precisely because Este power was in terminal decline by the beginning of the 16th century. Reading and listening to Ariosto's poem, the noblemen of Este could fantasize about defeating Turks, the latter-day equivalent of Saracens, but this was a purely aesthetic fantasy. By the 16th century, real imperial power lay outside Italy.

Luís de Camões's epic poem *The Lusiads* (1572) returned to a more immediate past, the fading glory of another European power, the Portuguese Empire. Camões was a soldier and imperial administrator who composed his poem as he worked in Africa, India, and Macau in the mid-16th century. *The Lusiads* mythologized the rise of the 15th-century Portuguese Empire by focusing on the voyage of Vasco da Gama to India in 1497. Like

Ariosto, Camões claimed his epic exceeded the ancients because its heroic and geographical scope – the deeds and exploits of the Portuguese in places never discovered by the Greeks or Romans – surpassed the achievements of the classical world. Camões sang 'of the famous Portuguese / To whom both Mars and Neptune bowed'. The poem created a literary template for literary imperialism, and was imitated throughout the 18th and 19th centuries of European global colonisation. However, by the 1570s when Camões wrote his epic, the Portuguese Empire was already in decline, and in 1580 the Spanish King Philip II annexed it as part of the expanding Habsburg Empire. As with Ariosto, Camões's poem was already trading on past glories.

In England, Edmund Spenser and Sir Philip Sidney took up the epic tradition but gave it a peculiarly Protestant sensibility. Both men were ambitious Elizabethan courtiers, eager to secure their own political positions by writing epics in line with the prevailing tastes of the Tudor dynasty. Sidney's *Arcadia* (1590) mixed narrative prose with pastoral verse spoken by Arcadian shepherds and disguised aristocratic heroes to address a range of issues central to the Elizabethan polity, from political counsel to the need to practise temperance and master the passions in matters of romance and dynastic alliances. Edmund Spenser was a political administrator, like both Ariosto and Camões, but his epic creation celebrated an empire that did not even exist. Spenser wrote *The Faerie Queene* (1590–6) while enthusiastically colonizing Ireland on behalf of his English sovereign, Queen Elizabeth I, the 'Goddesse heuenly bright, / Mirrour of grace and Maiestie diuine, / Great Lady of the greatest Isle'.

In deliberately archaic English Spenser follows the adventures of a series of individuals personifying specifically Protestant values, such as faith and temperance. He turns Elizabeth into a glorious 'Faerie Queen', and reclaims St George from his eastern origins as the patron saint of England. But this was another glorious myth. By the time Spenser completed his poem, Elizabeth was politically isolated in Europe and her only lasting colonial legacy was to have set the scene for subsequent centuries of sectarian violence in Ireland. Nevertheless, in creating an international epic in the vernacular on the birth of the Protestant English nation, Spenser turned away from the more mainstream European tradition, and heavily influenced Milton's *Paradise Lost*.

Theatre

Shakespeare's drama is a fitting place to conclude this survey of the Renaissance because his career marks a decisive shift from the classical, humanist tradition, that drew its strength from southern European and Mediterranean influences, to the more local and national preoccupations that signalled the end of the Renaissance. In his earliest plays Shakespeare remained deeply indebted to this classical tradition. In *The Comedy of Errors* (1594), Shakespeare rewrote the Roman playwright Plautus' comedy *Manaechmi*, setting it in classical Ephesus. His first foray into historical tragedy, *Titus Andronicus*, was similarly indebted to Roman history. The play tells the story of the struggle of the empire in its declining years through the character of Titus Andronicus, who watches the 'barbaric' Goths gradually infiltrate and overwhelm the 'civilized' values of Rome.

Although both these early plays show Shakespeare's debt to the classical past, they also reflect specific Elizabethan concerns and preoccupations. The comedy of mistaken identity and financial confusion in *Comedy of Errors* performs a growing English unease with the liquidity of money and the complexities of long-distance commercial transactions at a time when England was entering international markets in the Muslim-controlled Mediterranean. *Titus Andronicus* also shows Shakespeare writing a history of the pastness of the past, and trying to come to terms with English encounters with different cultures, personified in the attractive but sinister figure of Aaron the Moor, a precursor of Othello.

Shakespeare's growing confidence with historical sources led to an increased interest in more local, specifically Elizabethan issues in his subsequent comedies and histories. His cycle of history plays from *Richard II* to *Henry V* began to move from religiously inspired chronicle history to a more ambiguous and contingent understanding of England's recent past and its relationship to the present. Although these plays have been traditionally regarded as providing the Tudor state with an ideological justification of its political legitimacy, they also disclosed the cycle of bloody violence and usurpation undertaken by Queen Elizabeth's forebears. There is evidence that *Richard II* was performed in support of an unsuccessful coup against Elizabeth, and that *Henry V* was censored for its sensitive references to political difficulties in Ireland and Scotland.

The comedies reflect the growing linguistic confidence expressed in Shakespeare's sonnets. In *Twelfth Night*, Feste the clown tells the cross-dressed, Viola 'A sentence is but a cheveril glove to a good wit: how quickly the wrong side may be turned outward!' (*Twelfth Night*, 3. 1). The ability to turn language inside out, and argue for and against a particular position was an inheritance of humanist rhetoric, but in the commercial theatre of Elizabethan London, such techniques were used to perform and enact issues of direct relevance to the play's audience, be they rich or poor. The first Shakespearean play at the new Globe Theatre, *Julius Caesar*, returned to the classical past in its dramatization of the fall of the Roman republic with the assassination of Julius Caesar. But it also explored how rhetoric shaped political action. The legacy of republicanism, discussed in the contrasting funeral orations of Brutus and Mark Antony, was a potentially dangerous subject to discuss within the context of Elizabethan absolutism. However, as with many of the comedies, Shakespeare is more interested in how rhetoric shapes and persuades an audience, rather than endorsing a particular political ideology. The hopes and fears of an agrarian society struggling to adapt to a credit economy, the concerns of the status of women and changing familial relations, and the ever-present religious concerns of political authority and personal salvation were all recurrent issues that shaped Shakespeare's dramatic career.

'He was not of an age, but for all time.' This was Ben Jonson's epitaph on the death of his great rival, Shakespeare. Today, many would agree that Shakespeare's great tragic heroes – Hamlet, Macbeth, Lear, and Othello – are indeed enduring creations that transcend the time and place of their creation. But we should remember that a defining feature of the Renaissance is the ability of its greatest artists to self-fashion a belief in the timelessness of their work. As much as Hamlet is the quintessential Renaissance man, a complex, multifaceted harbinger of modernity who prefigures the insights of Marx and Freud, he was created amidst the particular pressures and anxieties of Shakespeare's time. It is easy to see his introspective speeches on death, and his puzzling inability to avenge the murder of his father, as reflecting the hopes and fears of every modern, alienated male teenager. However, it is important to understand that his actions were also shaped by England's reformed Protestant sensibilities, and the consonant fears concerning salvation and the afterlife, 'the undiscover'd country from whose bourn / No traveller returns'. Similarly, whilst Othello's murder of Desdemona appears to be a timeless reflection on the corrosive, and potentially fatal consequences of jealousy, it is also an exploration of Othello as an outsider, 'an extravagant and wheeling stranger / Of here and every where', a Muslim convert to Christianity familiar to those Englishmen openly trading with Morocco and the Islamic Ottoman Empire.

The Tempest provides a fitting conclusion to Shakespeare's career, and to this study of the Renaissance. Traditionally the play has been regarded as a meditation on the power of art, and represents Shakespeare's farewell to the stage. It is also one of Shakespeare's most classical plays. The action takes place in one day on the island, and its action draws on Virgil's *Aeneid*; Alonso the King of Naples is sailing home from Tunis, where he has married off his daughter

Claribel. Shipwrecked on Prospero's island somewhere in the Mediterranean, the voyage draws on Aeneas' journey from Troy to Rome via Carthage. However, the play also contains powerful associations with European colonization of the New World of America. The play looks both ways, to the eastern Mediterranean and the classical world that provided such a rich source of inspiration for Renaissance thinkers and artists, and westwards to the Atlantic world that would increasingly shape later 17th- and 18th-century Enlightenment thinking. If this shift in the literary, intellectual, and international outlook signalled the end of what defined the Renaissance, it also offered the beginning of a different, definably modern understanding of culture and society.

Timeline

1497–8	Da Gama reaches India
1500	Cabral lands in Brazil
1505	Leonardo, *Mona Lisa*; Dürer in Italy
1506	Bramante begins work on St Peter's, Rome
1509	Accession of King Henry VIII in England (rules until 1553)
1511	Erasmus, *Praise of Folly*
1512	Michelangelo completes Sistine Chapel ceiling; Erasmus, *De Copia*.
1513	Cortes in Mexico; Portuguese capture Hormuz; Machiavelli, *The Prince*
1515	Accession of King Francis I in France (rules until 1547)
1516	Charles V king of Spain; Erasmus's Greek New Testament; More, *Utopia*
1517	Luther's 95 theses
1520	Accession of Sultan Süleyman the Magnificent
1521	Diet of Worms; Magellan's expedition reaches the Pacific
1524	Peasant's Revolt in Germany; Raphael, *Donation of Constantine*
1525	Battle of Pavia; Dürer, *A Course in the Art of Measurement*
1527	Sack of Rome
1529	Treaty of Saragossa; Diogo Ribeiro world map
1533	Henry VIII splits with Rome; Holbein, *The Ambassadors*, Regiomontanus, *On Triangles*
1543	Copernicus, *De Revolutionibus*; Vesalius, *Fabrica*; Portuguese reach Japan
1545	Council of Trent begins (ends 1563)
1554	Bandello, *Novelle*
1555	Peace of Augsburg; Pope Paul IV's anti-Jewish papal bull; Labé, *Euvres*
1556	Abdication of Charles V; Philip II becomes king of Spain; Tartaglia, *A General Treatise on Numbers and Measurement*; Agricola, *De Re Metallica*
1558	Accession of Queen Elizabeth I in England
1567	Whitney, *The Copy of a Letter*
1569	Mercator's world map

1570	Elizabeth I excommunicated; Ortelius, *Theatrum Orbis Terrarum*
1571	Defeat of Ottoman naval forces at the Battle of Lepanto
1572	St Bartholomew's Day Massacre; Camões, *The Lusiads*
1580	Montaigne, *Essays*
1590	Spenser, *The Faerie Queene*
1603	Shakespeare, *Othello*; death of Elizabeth I; accession of James I
1604	Cervantes, *Don Quixote*
1605	Bacon, *Advancement of Learning*

Further reading

Introduction

Hans Baron, *The Crisis of the Early Italian Renaissance* (Princeton, 1955)

Warren Boutcher, 'The Making of the Humane Philosopher: Paul Oscar Kristeller and Twentieth-Century Intellectual History', in John Monfasani (ed.), *Kristeller Reconsidered* (New York, 2005), pp. 37–67

Jacob Burckhardt, *The Civilisation of the Renaissance in Italy*, tr. S. G. C. Middlemore (London, 1990)

W. K. Ferguson, *The Renaissance in Historical Thought: Five Centuries of Interpretation* (New York, 1970)

Mary S. Hervey, *Holbein's Ambassadors, the Picture and the Men: An Historical Study* (London, 1900)

Paul Oscar Kristeller, *The Philosophy of Marsilio Ficino* (New York, 1943)

Walter Mignolo, *The Darker Side of the Renaissance* (Ann Arbor, 1995)

Erwin Panofsky, *Studies in Iconology: Humanist Themes in the Art of the Renaissance* (Oxford, 1939)

Chapter 1

Ezio Bassani and William Fagg, *Africa and the Renaissance* (New York, 1988)

Jerry Brotton and Lisa Jardine, *Global Interests: Renaissance Art between East and West* (London, 2000)

Charles Burnett and Anna Contadini (eds.), *Islam and the Italian Renaissance* (London, 1999)

Deborah Howard, *Venice and the East* (New Haven, 2000)

Halil Inalcik, *The Ottoman Empire: The Classical Age 1300–1600*, tr. Colin Imber and Norman Itzkowitz (New York, 1973)

Gülru Necipoglu, 'Süleyman the Magnificent and the Representation of Power in the Context of Ottoman–Hapsburg–Papal rivalry', *Art Bulletin*, 71 (1989), 401–27

Julian Raby, *Venice, Dürer and the Oriental Mode* (London, 1982)

Chapter 2

Elizabeth Eisenstein, *The Printing Press as an Agent of Change*, 2 vols. (Cambridge, 1979)

Lucian Febvre, *The Coming of the Book*, tr. David Gerard (London, 1976)

Anthony Grafton and Lisa Jardine, *From Humanism to the Humanities: Education and the Liberal Arts in Fifteenth- and Sixteenth-Century Europe* (London, 1986)

William Ivins, *Prints and Visual Communications* (Cambridge, Mass., 1953)

Lisa Jardine, *Erasmus, Man of Letters* (Princeton, 1993)

Jill Kraye (ed.), *The Cambridge Companion to Renaissance Humanism* (Cambridge, 1996)

Chapter 3

John Bossy, *Christianity in the West, 1400–1700* (Oxford, 1985)

Thomas Brady *et al.* (eds.), *Handbook of European History, 1400–1600*, vol. 1 (Leiden, 1994)

Euan Cameron, *The European Reformation* (Oxford, 1991)

David M. Luebke (ed.), *The Counter-Reformation* (Oxford, 1999)

Steven Ozment, *The Age of Reform, 1250–1550* (New Haven, 1980)

Eugene Rice, *The Foundations of Early Modern Europe*, rev. edn. (New York, 1993)

Chapter 4

Jerry Brotton, *Trading Territories: Mapping the Early Modern World* (London, 1997)

Mary Baines Campbell, *Wonder and Science* (New York, 1999)

Tony Grafton, *New Worlds, Ancient Texts* (New York, 1995)

Jay Levenson (ed.), *Circa 1492: Art in the Age of Exploration* (Washington, 1992)

J. H. Parry, *The Age of Reconnaissance* (London, 1963)

Joan-Pau Rubies, *Travel and Ethnology in the Renaissance* (London, 2000)

Chapter 5

Marie Boas, *The Scientific Renaissance 1450–1630* (London, 1962)

Brian Copenhaver and Charles B. Schmitt, *Renaissance Philosophy* (Oxford, 1992)

Nancy Siraisi, *Medieval and Early Renaissance Medicine* (Chicago, 1990)

Quentin Skinner, *The Foundations of Modern Political Thought* (Cambridge, 1978)

Pamela H. Smith, *The Body of the Artisan* (Chicago, 2004)

Chapter 6

Terence Cave, *The Cornucopian Text* (Oxford, 1979)

Walter Cohen, *Drama of a Nation* (New York, 1985)

Margaret Ferguson *et al.* (eds.), *Rewriting the Renaissance* (Chicago, 1986)

Stephen Greenblatt, *Renaissance Self-Fashioning: From More to Shakespeare* (Chicago, 1980)

Ann Rosalind Jones, *The Currency of Eros: Women's Love Lyric in Europe, 1540–1620* (Bloomington, 1990)

David Quint, *Epic and Empire* (Princeton, 1993)

Index

A

absolutism 54–5, 125
accounting 27
Acre 24
Adorno, Theodor 17
Africa and Africans 21, 37, 61, 62, 73, 74, 79, 104, 122
  craftsmen 36, 37
  exploration of 81, 83–4
  slave trade 96
  trade 34–7, 83
Agricola's *De Re Metallica* 104
Alberti, Leon Battista 11, 45–6, 47–8, 67
Aleppo 23, 24
Alexander the Great 29, 87
Alexandria, Egypt 21, 23, 30, 34, 79, 81
Alfonso, King of Aragon 58, 59
algebra 26, 101
Alpago, Andrea 106
alum 104
amber 90
Amirutzes, Georgius 106, 107
anamorphosis 8
anatomy 99, 101, 102, 103, 108–9
anthropology 15, 17
anti-Semitism 16, 17, 27, 74
Antwerp 72
Arabs 7, 83, 87, 89, 126
  astronomy 99
  business practice 25–7
  manuscripts 62
  navigators 81, 86

science 105, *see also* Islam
architecture 62
  Alexandria 21
  east-west influences 24, 31, 33
  in Istanbul 29
  Portuguese 83
  in Rome 67
Aristo, Ludovico 122, 123
Aristotle 38, 62, 105, 110, 112, 113–14
arithmetic 3, 26, 46, 101
Armenians 61, 62
art 9
  Bellini's *Saint Mark Preaching in Alexandria* 19–21
  dyes 23
  east-west influences 30–2
  historians 9, 14, 24
  Holbein's *The Ambassadors* 1–8, 16
  Islamic 22
  realism 13–14
  religious 65–6, 74–5, 76
  and science 108
  self-fashioning 16
  'vulgarization' 66
  Walter Pater 12
artillery 103
Asia 33, 84, 92, 104
astronomy 3, 7, 51, 83, 86–7, 99, 100, 101, 106–7, 108
Austria 72
Averroës 110
Avicenna 105, 110
Azores 83, 84
Aztec Empire 93

Visit the
VERY SHORT
INTRODUCTIONS
Web site

www.oup.co.uk/vsi

➤ **Information** about all published titles

➤ News of **forthcoming books**

➤ **Extracts** from the books, including titles not yet published

➤ **Reviews** and views

➤ **Links** to other **web sites** and main OUP web page

➤ Information about **VSIs in translation**

➤ **Contact** the editors

➤ **Order** other **VSIs** on-line